The J.E. Dunn Story

"Anyone can build a building, but if you're going to stay in the building business, it's a matter of whether the client is happy or unhappy when the job is completed."

— Ernie Dunn Sr.

A baseball player with knowledge of construction, John Ernest "Ernie" Dunn Sr., founded J.E. Dunn Construction Company in the mid-1920s. Beginning with work on houses and apartments, J.E. Dunn was soon building schools, hospitals, Catholic churches and office buildings. During World War II, Ernie gained national attention when he refused any profit on government contracts, citing an unwillingness to profit from a war in which Americans – including his two sons – were risking their lives.

After Ernie died in 1964, his two sons, Ernie Jr. and Bill, ran the family business until 1974, when Bill bought out Ernie. Landing ever larger projects, the company continued in its founder's tradition by committing a percentage of its profits to charitable organizations in the Kansas City area. Over the second half of the century, countless organizations benefited from J.E. Dunn's generosity.

J.E. Dunn has not only established itself as a local, regional, and even national leader in building schools, churches, hospitals, prisons, offices, and high-tech buildings, but has served as a leader in equal opportunity employment and labor-management relations.

Since 1990, J.E. Dunn has brought other firms from Oregon to Georgia and from Minnesota to Texas under its expanding umbrella. Today the company ranks as the 11th largest general contractor in the United States and among the top 25 worldwide.

Most importantly, it has remained privately owned with four of Bill's five sons – Bill Jr., Terry, Steve, and Bob – at the helm.

Both employees and clients have remarked that J.E. Dunn "builds from the heart." That phrase captures the legacy Ernie Dunn began and that the third and now fourth generation of Dunns is carrying into the 21st century.

On the cover: J.E. Dunn Construction Company built the three tallest buildings in the photograph on the front cover: the two American Century Towers in Kansas City and the Marriott Plaza Hotel to the right.

The J.E. Dunn Story

BUILDING FROM THE HEART

By Kevin Dunn and Troupe Noonan

A HERITAGE HISTORIES BOOK

Photolab: Fotografix, Chapel Hill, N.C.
          Pixel Clear, Inc., Bellefonte, Pa.
Designed by Snavely Associates, Ltd., State College, Pa.
Printed by Rapid Solutions Group, Kansas City, Mo.

ISBN: 0-9752771-0-3

First Edition

Printed and Bound in the United States of America

10 9 8 7 6 5 4 3 2 1

Published by Heritage Histories
103 Sandy Creek Trail
Chapel Hill, N.C. 27514

The J.E. Dunn Story
BUILDING FROM THE HEART

Contents

You may hear some writers complain about their lonely profession, but not me. This book was a group effort from the start when my father, Bill Dunn Sr., called together J.E. Dunn consultant Meg Winch, J.E. Dunn employees Julie Ann Sturm and Sabra Sandy, and myself in early 2001 to write a company history. Meg may be the most effective multi-tasker I've ever met. Despite her involvement in many other projects at the time, Meg led us in coming up with an overall structure for the book and made the interview assignments. During the next several months, Julie Ann, Sabra, Meg, consultant Peter Hansen, and I interviewed scores of people for the book: construction company clients, subcontractors, current employees, retired employees, and Dunn relatives.

Julie Ann shined as an interviewer. Her questions got many J.E. Dunn superintendents to open up about how their jobs have changed over the years and how the construction business in general has changed. Thanks to all the people who allowed us to interview them. We learned so much from you. What quotes you see in the book represent just a fraction of what we gleaned from the interviews.

About a year into the project, my father decided to turn the writing of the book entirely over to me (Gulp!) I envy prolific writers who can crank out pages by the hour. Unfortunately, that didn't happen with this book. After inching my way through most of the first three chapters of the book, I wised up. Early in 2003, I telephoned a firm that specializes in developing corporate histories, Heritage Histories of Chapel Hill, N.C., headed up by Tim Troupe Noonan. In a matter of months, Heritage Histories wrote the last three chapters of the book, the epilogue, and several of the sidebars. They also packaged the book, selecting and overseeing editors, designers, printers, and binders and generally managed the project through to completion.

Many thanks go to everyone who helped to edit the book including Ardyth Wendte, Bernard Jacquinot, Ed Matheny, my brothers, and my father, in particular. Thanks to Snavely Associates for excellent design work and Rapid Solutions for printing and binding services, Julie Ann who continued to help Tim and me in finding photographs for the book, to Sabra for her help and encouragement throughout the process, and to many other J.E. Dunn employees for their assistance — Scott Kelly, Liz Nace, Barb Hachey, and Kathy Wehmueller, to name a few.

— **Kevin Dunn**

J.E. Dunn

FOREWORD

J. E. "Ernie" Dunn was born in 1893 and died in 1964. This book attempts to shed light on the life of the founder of J.E. Dunn Construction Company, his philosophy of doing business, and his legacy that continues today.

At all times he embraced the motto of the Associated General Contractors of "Quality, Economy, Integrity, and Performance." He even went further than the motto by his treatment of clients, designers, subcontractors, material suppliers, and his employees. His legacy of hiring the most qualified people and rewarding them for their efforts has been the spark that translated to the success of the company.

My father was devoted to his family, as well as the community. He never sought publicity for his philanthropy, and his philosophy of doing business is being faithfully adhered to by the employees of the company he founded.

– William H. Dunn Sr.

Chapter 1
THE FOUNDATION FOR THE FUTURE
1923-1945

Ernie Dunn, age 15, poses with his baseball team in 1909.

BUILDING A LIFE

J.E. Dunn

CHANGE IS GOOD, WE'RE TOLD. FOR THE J.E. DUNN CONSTRUCTION COMPANY, CHANGE HAS MEANT SURVIVAL. IF JOHN ERNEST DUNN SR. COULD SEE THE COMPANY NOW, HE'D BE AMAZED AT ITS GROWTH SINCE HE BEGAN THE BUSINESS IN KANSAS CITY, MO., IN THE 1920S. HE WOULD BE PROUD TOO THAT DESPITE ALL THE CHANGES, THE BEST TRADITIONS OF THE COMPANY REMAIN INTACT. THE COMPANY STILL BEARS THE STAMP OF ITS TOUGH BUT GENEROUS FOUNDER.

(left) Downtown Kansas City in the early 1920s.

(above) Ernie Dunn at age 24 in 1917, the year before he married Rose Bruening.

Almost everyone who knew J.E. Dunn Sr., or "Ernie," recalls how tough he could be. Retired superintendent Dick Neumann remembers Ernie Sr. at a jobsite, asking a construction worker what the driver on a bulldozer was doing. "Leveling off the ground," the construction worker told him. "Looks like he's just pushing my dollar bills around. Get him off the job until we're ready for him!" Mary Ellen, Ernie's oldest daughter, also recalls overhearing one of his outbursts. His voice boomed through the hallway at the company's former offices in the Reliance Building at 10th and McGee. "He was shouting on the phone at a subcontractor whose office was on Walnut, a few blocks over. The subcontractor snapped back, 'If you yell a little louder, you won't need to use the telephone!' "

Though a tough-minded businessman, Ernie also had a big heart. Friends and family didn't learn about one of his acts of kindness until 1965, a year after his death, when the *Kansas City Star* printed a letter from a principal from the former Humboldt School. The principal wrote about how

J.E. Dunn Sr. had helped pay for clothing and school materials for children at the elementary school at 11th and Holmes, one block south of the company's headquarters and not far from where Ernie grew up. "Mr. Dunn visited the school frequently, becoming acquainted with the teachers and the children, and familiarized himself with the problems that confronted us… He sent a monthly check to use as my staff and I thought best for the children."[1] Ernie only asked that his support for the school be kept a private matter between him and the school.

An Irish-Catholic Upbringing

*I*n many ways Ernie was a typical man of his era. He grew up at a time when the United States was still a young country, made up largely of immigrants. His own parents, William Thomas Dunn and Ellen Fitzgerald Dunn, came from working class Irish-Catholic families on Prince Edward Island in Canada. His father had a knack for woodworking and emigrated with his new bride to Ogden, Utah, in the late 1870s to become a carpenter for the Union Pacific Railroad.

The Reliance Building stood at 10th and McGee in downtown Kansas City. The J.E. Dunn office was on the fifth floor of the building until 1949.

William Thomas Dunn, a carpenter for the Union Pacific Railroad, moved his wife and children to Kansas City in 1880.

The family settled in Kansas City in 1880 when the railroad sent William to work as a carpenter foreman on the Union Depot in the West Bottoms. The International Brotherhood of Carpenters would posthumously honor William T. Dunn for his fine workmanship with a plaque hung in Kansas City's Union Station in the year 2001. More than a century earlier, John Ernest Dunn was born in Kansas City on June 5, 1893, the sixth of the carpenter's seven children.

Times were often tough for the family. The oldest son and oldest daughter both died in childhood from pneumonia. Ernie himself nearly died at the age of six when a streetcar ran over him, fracturing his skull in 57 places. He lay comatose in a hospital for six days before regaining consciousness. The accident left him with a deep scar that ran the length of his head. He trained with the Army for three months at Camp Funston in Kansas during World War I but was denied service in the Army Signal Corps after a military doctor got a closer look at the scar hidden under his hairline. The same war forever changed his favorite brother, Richard, who was exposed to mustard gas during combat and suffered lifelong tics.

Ernie tried to stay close to Richard, his other brothers, and his surviving sister throughout their adult lives. He helped them with employment and cash and built a house for his widowed mother, long after he had a wife and children of his own to support. His commitment to the family never wavered; he was known to hold a grudge against anyone who did them harm. His daughter, Rosalie, remembers how decades later Ernie would rant about the doctor who contributed to his father's death by mistaking the symptoms of a ruptured appendix for a stomachache and sending him home to die.

School and Baseball

*O*n the other hand, Ernie had nothing but praise for the doctor who saved his own life after the streetcar accident. Miraculously, the injury didn't have any lasting effects on him physically or mentally.

He went to the neighborhood parish school, St. Patrick's, in downtown Kansas City. In 1909, he graduated from St. Benedict's, a Catholic preparatory school for boys in Atchison, Kan. Academic records show that he made the honor roll in several of his classes including mathematics, his best subject.

Although he excelled in school, Ernie was hardly the reserved, bookish type. Photographs of him from this era show a determined young man who was built more like a bouncer than a scholar.

After high school, he was a pitcher for semiprofessional baseball leagues in the Midwest. The emotions could run high when Ernie took the mound. In one game, a young man about the same age as Ernie – 19 or 20 years old – razzed his pitching. The man, who happened to be the son of the opposing team's owner, continued jeering for five or six innings, until Ernie pulled him out of his front row seat and decked him. Then Ernie threatened to take on anyone else who was looking for a fight. As everyone in the stands rose to meet the challenge, he raced toward the center field fence to make a quick escape – one of the rare instances in his life when he ran from a fight.

Professional baseball players weren't a wealthy bunch in those days. Semipro players were paid even less, but they could make a little extra money by hiring themselves out for tournament games after the regular season ended. Weekend betting could add even more to the cash pile. Ernie would get $25 to play center field on a Saturday and then bet it all when he pitched on Sunday. One Sunday afternoon in rural Kansas, the betting didn't pay off. His team faced the pitcher, Walter "Big Train" Johnson, whose fastball would make him famous in baseball history. Ernie couldn't even see the baseball when Johnson hurled it across the plate.

(left) Maria and Henry Bruening, Rose Bruening's parents.

(center) A teenaged Ernie Dunn, in the cardigan sweater, stands on the far right with his baseball team.

(right) The Bruening family home at 3800 Washington. Maria Bruening wanted the house either given to a charitable institution or torn down after her death. When she died in 1935, her children couldn't find an institution that wanted the building and had it razed.

He may never have won any games against "Big Train," but Ernie was good enough at pitching semiprofessionally to get the attention of Charles "Kid" Nichols, a future Hall of Fame pitcher. Nichols helped Ernie get a professional pitching position on the Portland Beavers, a farm team of the St. Louis Browns. A newspaper clipping from the March 26, 1916, edition of *The Oregonian* gives his nickname on the Portland team as "Busher."

His professional pitching days didn't last long. Ernie returned to semiprofessional baseball in Kansas City, but the course of his life took a different turn during an off-season while he was working as a salesman for Magee Electric, a lighting supply company in Kansas City.

Electricity in the Air

$\mathcal{E}$ lectricity was a relatively new invention for World War I America. Some Kansas Citians were just converting from gaslights to electricity in their homes. One of them, Maria Bruening, called Ernie to look at her house, a three-story Victorian mansion designed and built by her deceased husband, Henry Bruening.

Ernie made an immediate impression on Mrs. Bruening when the two met at the house on that late summer day in 1916. Mrs. Bruening's surroundings hadn't always been so lavish; her parents were poor Austrian immigrants who scraped by on what they could make from gardening, cooking, and cleaning. She may have felt an instant affinity with the well-spoken immigrant's son who wanted to improve his lot. Perhaps the young salesman won her trust when he argued that her choice of lighting fixtures was too extravagant –

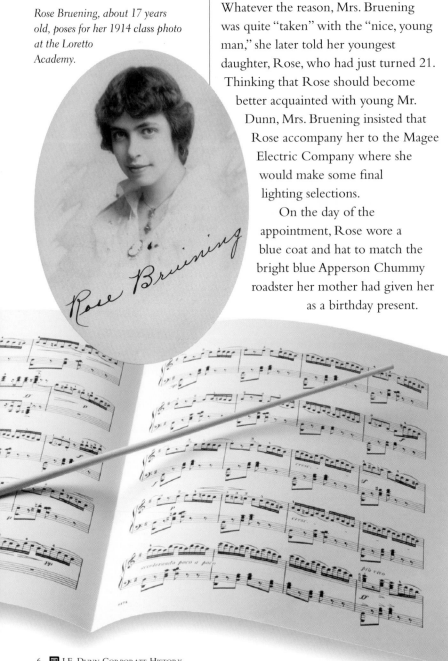

Rose Bruening

she shouldn't spend so much money. Whatever the reason, Mrs. Bruening was quite "taken" with the "nice, young man," she later told her youngest daughter, Rose, who had just turned 21. Thinking that Rose should become better acquainted with young Mr. Dunn, Mrs. Bruening insisted that Rose accompany her to the Magee Electric Company where she would make some final lighting selections.

On the day of the appointment, Rose wore a blue coat and hat to match the bright blue Apperson Chummy roadster her mother had given her as a birthday present.

Apparently, Ernie wasn't overwhelmed by her color coordination. He waited on the Bruening women in a businesslike manner without even glancing at Rose. His inattention didn't faze Rose; she went home without giving Ernest Dunn a second thought.

That November the house was wired for electricity and the lighting was installed. Then on the morning of December 31, 1916, Mr. Ernest Dunn stopped by "to check if the fixtures were working properly." Rose invited him inside. After making some small talk, Ernie asked her to a dance on New Year's Day at the Field Club where he played on the baseball team. Rose said yes, she had no plans for the next day, but let him know that she already had a date for New Year's Eve. They danced on January 1, 1917, and married a year and a half later on June 12, 1918. Some time between those two dates, Rose won out over baseball. After she saw Ernie get struck by a baseball during a game – he wasn't hurt seriously – Rose issued her ultimatum: "It's either baseball or me." Ernie's pitching days were over.

Mr. and Mrs. John Ernest Dunn must have seemed like an odd couple at times. Ernie was known for his quick wit and even quicker temper, while Rose was reserved, cultured, and even-tempered. Former J.E. Dunn employees remember how

impatient Ernie Sr. could be, raising a ruckus if a job fell behind schedule. He wanted the job done yesterday, workers recall. "Is there a bricklayers convention in town?" he once asked at a construction site. "It looks like they're starting one at the water barrel right now!" When his temper flared, his son, Bill, remembers, "He could swear like a trooper!"

Rose Dunn was her husband's opposite in temperament, but was no stick-in-the-mud. She was a classically trained pianist who banged out ragtime tunes at the piano in her free time. She liked to swim, loved to laugh – her husband could always get a smile out of her – and she didn't hold back at showing affection to the people she loved. Many of her grandchildren can attest to wiping Grandma's lipstick off their cheeks. Though her husband may have ruled at the construction site, Rose was the undisputed head of the household. She handled the disciplining of their four children who came along in short order: John Ernest Jr., "Ernie," was born March 21, 1919, then Mary Ellen on September 23, 1921, followed by William Henry "Bill" on July 20, 1923, and Rosalie on October 8, 1926. Rose, the enforcer, made sure that the children did their lessons as soon as they got home from school. No questions were asked when she assigned chores to each child, and her husband's temper was kept in check on the home front. "There was

Rose Dunn at home with her children (l-r) Rosalie, Mary Ellen, Bill, and Ernie.

never any dissension between my mother and father," says Bill.

From Marriage to Construction

Married life played a large role in Ernie's next round of career changes. In 1920, Ernie hired laborers to build his first house, a bungalow at 59th Street Terrace and Pennsylvania; he planned to move there with Rose and their baby boy, Ernie Jr. All during construction of the home, Mrs. Bruening, Rose's mother, lamented that Rose would be living too far away from her. When the house was nearly complete, Ernie decided to give in to his mother-in-law's wishes – he sold the bungalow at a profit of $2,500. Less than a year later, Mrs. Bruening showed her appreciation by loaning Ernie money to buy a bigger house. After Rose had their second child, Mary Ellen, the family moved to 3710 Jefferson, less than two blocks away from the Bruening house at 38th and Washington.

About this same time, Ernie bought a half-interest at his workplace and its name changed to Magee-Dunn Electric

The building that housed the Magee-Dunn Electric Company still stands today in the Brookside neighborhood of Kansas City.

Company. In 1921, Magee's brother bought out Ernie, who used the money to start Dunn Electric Company at 11th and McGee Streets. The electric business didn't hold his interest for long. Ernie built and sold two more houses before closing Dunn Electric and starting a construction company.

There are probably many good reasons why Ernie made the switch from an electrical supply business to construction. He may have foreseen the demand for lighting fixtures tapering off when most everyone had converted their buildings from gas lighting to electricity. Also, along with the rest of the country, Kansas City's economy was booming during the early and mid-1920s. Developer J.C. Nichols helped push the city's growth southward by opening the Plaza shopping district in 1924 and laying out neighborhoods even farther south along the trolley line and new roads. The demand for new housing showed no signs of slowing down. It was a prime time to jump into the construction business.

Ernie's in-laws may also have swayed him toward construction. Although Ernie never knew his father-in-law, Henry Bruening, who died in 1915, he may have been inspired by his in-law's success in construction. The son of a German cabinetmaker, nineteen-year-old Henry followed his older brother, Theodore, to

America in 1870, and learned English and architecture in St. Louis. Theodore and Henry moved to Kansas City in the 1870s and ran a successful business: Bruening Brothers Contracting Company. Their company built several business buildings in downtown Kansas City, including the Warneke Building and the Western Star Building on Grand Avenue and the Muehlebach Brewery at 18th and Main. Henry was the architect on all of them.

Henry's successes weren't limited to designing and constructing buildings; he also was adept at buying and selling them. Ernie must have heard how Henry Bruening bought the family home at 2345 Baltimore for $8,000 and then sold it in 1901 for $32,000 to the Kansas City Terminal Company. Bruening Brothers Contracting Company financed the construction on several of its projects, making Henry and Theodore part owners and active investors in these properties. Their example may have shown Ernie that construction could be the means to an end: owning property.

Early J.E. Dunn Buildings

Ownership was Ernie's goal when he began work on the Belleview Hotel at 11th and Euclid. Ernie got the idea for the hotel from black carpenters and stonemasons who helped him build his first houses. They told him that the black community needed a hotel. When the three-story hotel was complete, he installed a manager and dragged Rose along for the opening even though she was due any day with their third child. It was the summer of 1923, the same year that Ernie's father, William, died suddenly. No one is alive now to say what influence William T. Dunn, the Union Pacific carpenter, had in his son's career path. It's easy to imagine Ernie bringing his father to the construction sites on the early jobs and asking his advice. Ernie and Rose named their baby boy after both of the grandfathers, William and Henry.

Some time around the birth of their third child, the J.E. Dunn Construction Company began to take shape. Ernie built a second, larger hotel, the Booker T. Washington, at 1821-23 Vine Street, in what is now considered to be the heart of Kansas City's historic jazz district. Many well-known entertainers of the era stayed there, including Cab Calloway and Bill "Bojangles" Robinson.

There isn't much known about the early years at J.E. Dunn Construction Company. Rose Dunn gave a few insights in the family history written in 1969. For example, she wrote about the Belleview and Booker T. Washington hotels. But she doesn't pinpoint the year the construction company officially opened.

The West Height Apartments, one of J.E. Dunn Construction's first buildings, built in Kansas City, Kan., in 1927.

(left) *The residence of Mrs. E. Hackett was designed by architect A.W. Archer and built by J.E. Dunn.*

(right) *Ernie Dunn built this house for his wife's nephew, Victor Zahner. The architect was Joseph B. Shaughnessy.*

The 1930s and Early 1940s

*T*he construction industry took a direct hit when the stock market crashed in October 1929. The company had only been in business about six years when the Great Depression saw the demand for new business buildings and luxury homes shrink overnight. The private sector that had fueled much of the J.E. Dunn company growth in the 1920s was hurting. In the Midwest, the climate was as grim as the economic outlook. Before anyone had ever heard of global warming, the Plains states baked under 100-degree heat waves that lasted for weeks. Kansas Citians could literally taste the Dust Bowl when west winds blew in dirt and grit from parched fields hundreds of miles away.

Both the list of J.E. Dunn clients and the size of the jobs were small in the early 1930s. For example, the company built the Winters Service Station in Kansas City, Kan., for $3,000 in 1931.

One of the earliest references, the January 1944 edition of *Architecture and Design* magazine, gives 1922 as the year it started. Some sources state that the company began in 1923, others say 1924.

A great deal of the company's early work consisted of homebuilding. One of Bill Dunn's earliest memories is the building of the next Dunn family home at 54th and Central, near Loose Park. Bill was only three years old at the time, but he remembers his father's company using a team of horses to haul dirt so the basement walls could be built.

Scheduling wasn't always Ernie's strong suit. Rose's mother suffered a serious stroke the morning of the move-in date, and later that morning Rose went into labor while the movers were bringing furniture into the house. Maria Bruening survived the stroke and had a new granddaughter, Rosalie, by the next morning, October 8, 1926.

The building and completion of other J.E. Dunn houses wasn't usually so eventful. Most were large, traditionally styled houses such as the two brick Tudor residences built for Mrs. E. Hackett and Mr. Victor Zahner. The new business was staying well afloat, but homebuilding probably lost its luster for Ernie when some homeowners began stalling in their payments.

The company branched out into other areas of construction. The company built two fire stations in Kansas City and did remodeling work at three others. Bill remembers one of the fire chiefs, Frank O'Connor, who would stop by the house to visit. J.E. Dunn also built the West Height Apartments in Kansas City, Kan., a structure to which he would add an addition in the 1940s. And then, not more than six years after the company started, the Great Depression hit.

Ernie moved the company from 11th and McGee to 55th and Brookside, where he opened a paint store to supplement the construction business. Either Ernie didn't have much luck selling paint or he was oversupplied in inventory, but years later his daughter Rosalie found stacks and stacks of unopened paint cans stashed in the basement of the family home. Mary Ellen says her parents never let on to her that times were hard, but she remembers her father scouting the neighborhoods looking for possible projects.

Church Work

Religious institutions and government-funded jobs gave the company the break it needed. Some of the help came from Atchison, the home of Ernie's high school alma mater. The Benedictine nuns at Mount St. Scholastica, the women's college in the town, hired Ernie and company to build a new dormitory and chapel at a cost of $300,000. Ernie caused a stir among the businessmen in Atchison when he paid his laborers 50 cents an hour instead of the established local rate of 30 cents an hour. He said he had figured 50 cents an hour for labor in the bid and that's what he intended to pay them. After construction was completed,

local merchants told the nuns to thank Mr. Dunn. Apparently, the laborers spent their extra pay in the shops of Atchison.

The town could also thank J.E. Dunn and a Milwaukee architecture firm, E. Brielmaier & Sons, for a beautiful and well-crafted chapel. Its limestone exterior featured a large rosette window high above the entryway, and the interior was bright and airy. In later decades, J.E. Dunn Construction would return to Atchison to do other construction work for the Catholic religious community, such as building the top floor of the Benedictine Fathers Abbey. More recently, J.E. Dunn completed extensive renovation work on the century-old freshman hall at Benedictine College and also built the student union on campus.

Benedictine College's rival, Rockhurst College (now Rockhurst University) in Kansas City, was another big customer of J.E. Dunn Construction in the mid-1930s. The Jesuit college needed a second building to house its classrooms and hired Dunn for the job. When Ernie saw that he was able to save $25,000 in its construction he applied the money to his next Rockhurst job: the Rockhurst field house. Ernie became a lifelong benefactor of both Benedictine and Rockhurst Colleges, but he didn't like to trumpet his generosity. When the president

The Rockhurst Field House was one of J.E. Dunn's earliest projects for the Jesuit college.

of Rockhurst College, Father Maurice Van Ackeren, asked that one of the campus buildings be named Dunn Hall in his honor, Ernie balked. "If you do that, this school will never get another dime from me," he said. Several years later, the building was named after Father Van Ackeren instead.

Work for other Catholic institutions followed the Benedictine and Rockhurst jobs. One of the larger religious projects completed before World War II was the Motherhouse of the Sisters of Charity in Leavenworth, Kan. The well-established religious order had taught school and ministered to the sick and poor in the region for nearly a hundred years when J.E. Dunn began the construction.

There was no shortage of downtrodden people for the good nuns to tend during the 1930s. Unemployment rates stayed high, and the breadline became a symbol for the national economy. The federal government tried to put people back to work with New Deal programs and funneled money into public works projects at state and local levels. Private contractors such as Ernie Dunn benefited.

Public Works

Some of the earliest relief came to J.E. Dunn Construction Company from a city-sponsored job. In 1933, Ernie turned in the lowest bid, $54,804, to build an addition at Kansas City's General Hospital No. 1. Later the same year, he was awarded an even larger job by the federal government. J.E. Dunn beat out 19 other contractors on a job to build 16 dwellings for employees at the Leavenworth Federal Penitentiary; Ernie's bid was $106,486. The government required Ernie to get bonding before it would award him the job. This was no easy task for a small contractor during the bleakest days of the Depression. On Ernie's first attempt, the Massachusetts Bonding & Insurance Co. denied his bonding request. In a letter to local insurance broker, Joseph McGee of Thomas

(above) Ernie Dunn, front, became good friends with his banker, Charlie Aylward. Later, their children would marry.

(right) A page from the J.E. Dunn's application to the Massachusetts Bonding Company lists the construction company assets.

McGee & Sons, Charles S. Clark of the bonding company explained why the request was denied: "The financial statement of this principal (J.E. Dunn) is far from satisfactory as he owes more than he has money in the bank... We must therefore ask that you write no further bonds for this principal without the consent of this office."

Ernie might have lost the Leavenworth job at this point were it not for the support of Joseph McGee and Kansas City banker Charlie Aylward. Less than a week after receiving Clark's letter, McGee wrote back to tell him that Thomas McGee & Sons would back J.E. Dunn with a $50,000 bond on the job – despite Clark's advice – and got a local surety company to act as

guarantor for half of the bond. Charlie Aylward, a vice president at the Columbia National Bank where Ernie owed money, may have swayed Joseph McGee's decision to bond the construction company. Aylward had earlier written to McGee: "We (at the bank) have been favored with an account from Mr. J.E. Dunn for a number of years, and the balances have at all times been satisfactory... We have a high regard for Mr. Dunn and believe that he is a very capable builder." Aylward assured McGee that the bank would loan money to the construction company on the Leavenworth job if Ernie needed it.

J.E. Dunn did remodeling work for the Swope Park Zoo in the 1930s.

Charlie Aylward and his wife, Dorothy, became good friends with Ernie and Rose. Their daughter, Jean Aylward, would eventually marry Ernie and Rose's son, Bill. But it wasn't love at first sight. When they were two kids in the same piano class in the early 1930s, Jean thought Bill Dunn was too smart for his own good.

After completing the federal job in Leavenworth, J.E. Dunn did more city-sponsored work, such as the remodeling of the Swope Park Zoo. This particular job had some unusual challenges, due in part to zoo director Tex Clark. A practical joker, Clark liked to scare people with the animals at the zoo. He told one J. E. Dunn laborer how to find his way to a cave at the zoo, but didn't mention that he'd be sharing the dark place with a caged lion. Another incident caused a laborer named Whitechild to believe the pranks went too far. One day, he felt

something scaly on his shoulder and looked back to see a big crocodile grinning at him less than an arm's length away. He had run some distance before realizing that Clark held the crocodile on a leash with its jaws clamped shut. Understandably, Whitechild threatened to quit and only returned to work when his safety could be reassured. With some luck, the J.E. Dunn crew managed to finish the zoo remodeling – psychologically traumatized perhaps, but alive and unbitten.

A Turning Point

*T*he next city job for J.E. Dunn, the Police Municipal Courts building in downtown Kansas City, marked a turning point for the construction company in several ways. For one, it was the biggest job J.E. Dunn had taken on to date, worth more than $900,000 by the time it opened in 1938. Its successful completion proved that J.E. Dunn could compete with "the big boys," such as Swenson Construction, the firm that had built City Hall and the Jackson County Courthouse. After the Police Municipal Courts job, journalists began using adjectives such as "prominent" and "experienced" when they wrote about J.E. Dunn in their newspapers.

The Police Municipal Courts building was also J.E. Dunn's most visible project to date. It was a city focal point at 12th

Because of the crude hoisting systems in use at the time, moving materials upward was a great challenge in the early part of the 20th century. Forklifts weren't around yet and cranes were unheard of. If something needed to be moved from the ground floor of a construction site to an upper story, wooden hoists and simple pulley systems were the only options.

Like the hoists, construction scaffolding and shoring were usually made of wood; they were far more unstable than the steel bracing in use today.

Workers on the Police Municipal Courts building, which was completed in 1938.

and Locust, sited at right angles to City Hall to the northwest and the Jackson County Courthouse to the southwest. Wight and Wight Architects designed it in the same sleek, art deco style as these two other buildings, but the Police Municipal Courts building stood on its own with shorter, more classic dimensions and a handsome, exterior clock that marked a central axis for this triad of government buildings. Kansas City wouldn't see another government building that matched them in grace and style until the end of the century, when J.E. Dunn Construction built the federal courthouse, two blocks north of City Hall.

The Police Municipal Courts building was constructed during the height of the Pendergast machine. Political boss Tom Pendergast called the shots at City Hall throughout the 1930s in Kansas City. Many years earlier, Ernie Dunn had played on a city league team sponsored by Pendergast. Though Pendergast liked the young Irishman, he advised Ernie never to ask a favor from him. Ernie never did seek Pendergast's help; he was awarded the Police Municipal Courts project by competitively outbidding six other contractors.

Ernie was especially proud of the Police Municipal Courts building, his son Bill remembers. Having such an impressive job under his belt may have been the boost Ernie needed to take on the many large projects that would soon come his way. For example, he helped expand several government-funded hospitals in the late 1930s and early 1940s, adding a central heating plant to General Hospital No. 1, a nurses' home at General Hospital No. 2, and an infirmary and dormitory at State Hospital No. 2 in St. Joseph, Missouri – a $688,000 project. It is a sad commentary on the times that the United States continued to be a segregated country in the 1930s: Kansas City's General Hospital No. 1 could only be used by white people while General Hospital No. 2 was the "blacks only" hospital. Institutional segregation wouldn't begin to lose its grip until after World War II, when President Truman integrated the Armed Forces.

One of the J.E. Dunn projects in this pre-World War II era looked back to an earlier war. J.E. Dunn Construction was commissioned to build a dedication wall at Liberty Memorial in Kansas City to commemorate people who had died during World War I. The wall was inscribed with quotes from President Woodrow Wilson and General John J. Pershing. About 60 years later, J.E. Dunn Construction

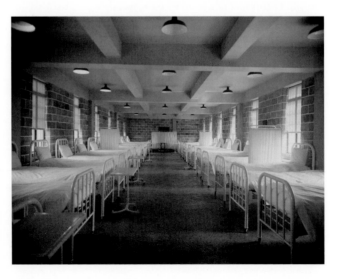

(far left) The tower at the Liberty Memorial.

(left) A wing of the infirmary at State Hospital No. 2 at St. Joseph, built in the 1930s.

(right) Bishop Lillis High School.

(above) An aerial view of Lincoln Park government-housing project in Denver.

(below) The St. Louis Housing Authority invites the public to see old housing demolished to make way for Carr Square Village.

Company would restore the war memorial and expand its museum space.

A significant amount of government money during the Depression years was also directed toward public education. The government allocated $600,000 for J.E. Dunn to consolidate three institutions in Kansas City: Manual High School, Lathrop Polytechnic Institute, and the Jane Hayes Gates Institute. After J.E. Dunn had connected the three structures, the resulting building was named Manual Training High School. The construction company also added several buildings to the Northwest Missouri State Teachers College at Maryville, built the Ott Grade School in Independence, and added twelve rooms to the Switzer School at 1829 Madison. The parochial school system kept the

construction crews busy, too. J.E. Dunn broke ground on building Bishop Lillis High School and erected a gymnasium for Visitation School where the Dunn children had attended grade school.

More city work came along when Dunn turned in the low bid to construct the Produce Buildings located in Kansas City's city market on 3rd Street, between Main and Walnut streets. The three one-story buildings, also called the Merchants' Buildings and the Kansas City Food Terminal, consisted of glass and brick construction. They still frame the city marketplace today. Built at the end of the art deco period, there is a hint of that style in their brickwork. When the 1940s arrived, architectural style lost out to a mandate for efficiency in government-funded construction: build it fast, build it cheaply, and forget the frills.

Ernie Dunn's company more than met the new criteria of building it "fast and cheap" when his company built two huge housing complexes during the early days of World War II: Carr Square Village in St. Louis and Lincoln Park in Denver. Both were city-authorized jobs that were begun in 1940 and funded by the United States Housing Authority. They were bigger than any jobs the construction company had done before; Carr

Square was a $2.5 million job and Lincoln Park was worth $1.5 million.

For Carr Square, St. Louis slums were torn down in a 12 square block area to make way for 54 two-story and three-story apartment buildings to house 658 low-income families. The local St. Louis newspaper touted the project as a "model housing project for Negroes." Government housing was as segregated as public hospitals at this time. The sturdy brick box-like buildings didn't win any awards for architectural design, but J.E. Dunn completed the work on time for the scheduled opening in the summer of 1942. The Denver job, Lincoln Park, included two- and three-story apartment buildings spread out over four square blocks. The *Rocky Mountain News* said the apartments "will be the last word in modernity" for the 346 low-income families for whom they were built. Ernie oversaw much of the construction and stayed in Denver for long periods to make sure the project kept on schedule. He didn't like being away from his family, however, and brought his wife and children to Denver with him whenever he could.

Work Hard, Play Hard

*I*t probably didn't surprise any of his children that Ernie Sr. would ask his family to join him in Denver. Nor did it surprise them later, when he would try to

You are invited to attend
Formal Ceremony
Celebrating demolition of old houses in blocks between WASH, BIDDLE, 15th and 18th Streets to clear way for New Construction of
CARR SQUARE VILLAGE
(658 Dwelling Units for Negro Families)
3 o'clock, Sunday, March 16th
CARR SQUARE PARK
15th and Carr Streets
House at 1023 Selby Place to be blown down by high pressure stream of water.
PROMINENT SPEAKERS
News Reels and Photographs will be taken
ST. LOUIS HOUSING AUTHORITY
W. C. CONNETT, Chairman

coax each of his sons and daughters into going to work for him.

"As far as our parents were concerned, we were the cat's meow," Mary Ellen recalls. Ernie Sr. never missed one of his oldest daughter's basketball games at Visitation Grade School or St. Teresa's Academy, coached Ernie Jr.'s, grade school baseball team, and was always an enthusiastic fan.

Ernie Sr. had his own group of fans among the neighborhood children. He used to come home from work with a sack full of candy for all of them. It is likely that he ate a sizeable chunk of the sweets himself. Though he never smoked, and drank alcohol infrequently, Ernie Sr. had a weakness for candy, especially chocolate, and it began to show. With his big belly, the bags of goodies, and what some people have called, "a twinkle in his eyes," Ernie was the Loose Park neighborhood's year-round Santa Claus – when he was in a good mood, anyway. As a little girl, youngest daughter Rosalie was afraid of her father because of his booming voice and his Irish temper. "It wasn't until I was older that I realized what a big teddy bear he was," Rosalie says.

Ernie Sr. could be a good sport, too. When the three older children would take turns beating him at ping-pong, their father would come back for more. When he would use the ping-pong table as a place to work on construction plans late into the night, however, they knew to stay quiet and out of sight.

The Dunn children understood early on that the home was also a second office for their father, and their mother, at times. Ernie relied on Rose to be his bookkeeper during the early days of his business. When the company officially became incorporated on December 2, 1928, Rose, who had grown up in a household where women were expected to know the basics of the business world, was listed as its secretary. Mary Ellen remembers her mother and grandmother going to some of their leased properties to collect the rent. Former J.E. Dunn employees remember seeing Rose at construction sites with Ernie, advising him on what color paint to use on property he planned to lease.

Rose's biggest contribution to the construction company was probably her willingness to put her own assets at risk when her husband needed a business loan from the bank or an approval for bonding. Rose had inherited money from her father, and both money and property when her mother died in 1935. In 1937, Rose's real estate holdings were mortgage-free and valued at $135,000, according to a financial statement the construction company submitted to the Central Surety and Insurance Corporation. Ernie did his best to minimize the financial risk to

Ernie was such a big fan of sports that he often proved to be a distraction to his children. It got to be too much for Bill while he was pitching a game for his high school baseball team.

"I'd have two balls on a batter and then hear my father yelling, 'Get the damn ball over the plate,'" says Bill. "Afterward, I told my dad that he could read about my games on the sports page or I would tell him about them, but I didn't want him to come to any more games. He agreed. I finished the season with a 13-win/2-loss pitching record. He kept coming to my high school and college football games, which was fine, because the crowds were loud enough to drown him out."

Bill Dunn, a hurler like his father, winds up to pitch for Rockhurst College baseball team.

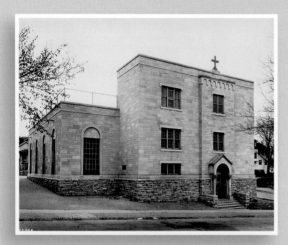

Blessed Sacrament School where Bill Dunn worked for Depression-era wages on his first construction job in summer 1941.

Bill Dunn, Sr. found that being the boss's son didn't hold any privileges. He has vivid memories of one of his early jobs, the building of a new Blessed Sacrament School at 39th and Agnes. "I'd just finished my freshman year at Rockhurst College when I worked on a construction job for the first time at Blessed Sacrament. It was Depression era wages that summer of 1941. Laborers made 55 cents an hour. My father couldn't afford to pay me that much; I was listed as a water boy and paid a dollar a day or 12 ½ cents an hour doing laborer's work."

his wife by taking out a life insurance policy to protect her property from creditors if he died. Still, he owed Rose a lot. During the Depression, Rose's financial backing helped the construction company qualify for jobs that might otherwise have been out of its reach.

With a marriage that was always an equal partnership, Ernie and Rose were ahead of their time. Ernie admired his wife's intelligence and must have envied her ability to keep a cool head. It may not have been official, but in many ways J.E. Dunn Construction Company was a family business right from the start, with Rose as her husband's closest advisor.

Ernie held his mother-in-law in the same high regard as his wife. When Rose remarked that her mother would have been such a brilliant woman if she could only have attended school a few more years, Ernie replied, "With her wisdom and philosophy of life, she doesn't need an education to be brilliant." At Ernie's insistence, they had Mrs. Bruening over for dinner every Thursday evening and visited her every Sunday until her death.

From the 1920s to the early 1940s, Ernie Sr. devoted most of his time to work and family. He spent any leftover time doing private charitable work, going to church, and socializing with a small circle of friends. He didn't join any boards until he became an officer and later president of the Builders'

Association of Greater Kansas City in the early 1940s. A printed program for the association's annual banquet dinner gave brief biographies of its board members. For hobbies, the other half-dozen male board members listed golf, hunting, or other activities a person could do alone or with one's buddies. By contrast, Ernie Sr. listed his hobbies as "helping boys," "baseball," "football," and "getting out into the country." His activities were either youth- or family-centered; he was a family man before it became popular.

For Ernie, "getting out to the country" usually meant taking his family to land that he'd bought in Stanley, Kan. – an area now part of Kansas City's vast suburban sprawl. The 40 acres of land consisted of a swimming pool, a fishing pond, fields that were leased for pasture, and a few small, unfurnished buildings, one of which had been converted into a two-bedroom cabin. Mary Ellen remembers going to the Stanley property nearly every day during some summers and making frequent weekend trips during the school year.

When a minor catastrophe occurred on the Stanley property, Ernie – the man who was supposed to have such a short fuse – proved how patient he could be when one of his children was partly to blame. In this case, his son, Bill, was the guilty party. Bill had mixed feelings about the country place because he did many of the chores there, such as pool cleaning and painting. One of his annual responsibilities was to burn off the brush and weeds in the grassy areas. The dried up stubble burned easily enough; the trick was to keep the fire under control. Late one afternoon, Bill and a friend thought they had the job licked. They let the fire advance toward them slowly until the entire field was burned and then smothered the flames with wet gunnysacks. They were ready to leave when Bill thought he saw the setting sun reflected in the windows of a storage building. A closer look showed a fire burning inside. The Stanley fire department came to the scene, but because there wasn't any way to bring water to the spot, the men just watched and listened to the popping fire engulf the wooden frame from the ground up.

To say that Ernie took the news calmly would be an understatement, but he didn't blow up at Bill. Someone did eventually get chewed out – the insurance agent when Ernie found out he'd let the policy lapse on the property. He got an earful.

When Ernie was able to leave his work at the office, he was happy at home. But the domestic tranquility was threatened whenever he had to work with his hands. Ernie, the carpenter's son, was, unfortunately, all thumbs when it came to building or

fixing things around the house. It was usually best to cover one's head and duck on the rare occasions that he tried to be handy. Bill remembers how his father's attempt at nailing together a birdhouse ended in profanity and a flying hammer. Usually, if any dexterity with tools was required for a chore at home, Ernie called in one of his construction workers, with one exception. "He liked to buy and fix antique clocks," Mary Ellen recalls, and when he was tinkering with one, "he had the patience of Job."

The Children Join the Company

*E*rnie's children learned not to expect that kind of patience when they joined him in the workplace. "When he took his hat off, you knew there was going to be trouble," Bill remembers. Ernie Jr. and Mary Ellen were just kids in the early 1930s when they became the cleaning crew at the office at 55th and Brookside. They cleaned on Saturdays and were each paid a dime – the ticket price at the nearby Plaza movie theater. The pay scale for Ernie Jr. improved somewhat in 1938. After attending Rockhurst College for two years, he began working for the construction company full time as a timekeeper and rose quickly through the ranks. When J.E. Dunn Construction started

The "business" side of J.E. Dunn required a different sort of effort in the first half of the 20th century. The adding machine was the only mathematical tool available at the time for preparing a bid. Calculators and computers were mere science fiction. Ernie Sr. did his fair share of crunching numbers then because nearly all his work before the war was hard bid.

Secretaries didn't have it easy either. The office stayed noisy with the clatter of secretaries pounding out business correspondence on their manual typewriters, and carbon copies were the most effective way to reproduce letters. With the great volume of typing required of their secretaries, the bosses were a little more lenient about typing errors than they might be today. Luckily, after the war, technological innovations made some aspects of their jobs a little easier for J.E. Dunn secretaries, even as their workload grew.

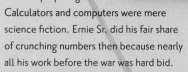

Rosalie wouldn't let her father lure her into the family business. She is shown here enrolling in medical technology courses for the fall 1947 semester at Webster College in St. Louis.

work on Bishop Lillis High School in Kansas City in August of 1940, Ernie Jr. was promoted to construction superintendent. Under his supervision, the company completed the $175,000 high school less than eight months later. By the start of World War II, 22-year-old Ernie was proving himself quite capable as second in command to his father, overseeing some of the construction company's largest public housing projects.

In 1939, Mary Ellen went to work as a receptionist for J.E. Dunn for $10 a week. The office had moved to the Reliance Building at 10th and McGee by this time. Mary Ellen remembers how businesslike her father was at work; the few other women who worked in office were always referred to as 'Miss Brennan' and 'Miss Mathews' – never by their first names. Mary Ellen had already graduated from St. Teresa's College but she attended the Sarachon Hooley School to learn typing, shorthand, and bookkeeping. The business courses prepared her to eventually become head bookkeeper for the company.

The 40-hour workweek hadn't exactly caught on at J.E. Dunn Construction.

Mary Ellen worked from 8 a.m. to 5:30 or 6 p.m. on weekdays – later when subcontractors came in late with their bids – and on Saturdays from 8 a.m. to 2 p.m. Payroll became one of her job duties: timekeepers would tell her the labor hours on Friday nights and she would work on the weekends so that paychecks would be ready on Monday morning. Mary Ellen remembers the payroll situation getting a little sticky on the Police Municipal Courts project: "The city didn't really have enough money to do the job" she recalls. "Dad had to borrow money from the bank each week just to pay everyone on the payroll. Dad didn't lose any money on that job, but he didn't make much either."

J.E. Dunn was involved in some large projects during the pre-war years but there were rarely more than three going on at any one time. Mary Ellen remembers her father visiting construction sites nearly every weekday morning, and construction foremen would report to the office every Saturday morning. Her father's close contact with his field operations gave Mary Ellen a deep appreciation for the people most responsible for the company's success. "My father's biggest strength in business was having some really good superintendents on the jobs, men like A.J. Timms and Harry Gilchrist, that he depended on a lot."

Out of all of their children, Ernie and Rose's youngest, Rosalie, showed the least

amount of interest in the family business. "I wanted to be a doctor but my mother and father did not think that was a proper profession for a young lady. They said I should be a nurse but I didn't want to." They reached a compromise. Rosalie enrolled in a five-year course in medical technology, spending her first two years at St. Teresa's College in Kansas City and completing the next three years at Webster College in St. Louis. After Rosalie finished a one-year internship at St. Mary's Hospital in Kansas City, her father made one last attempt to bring her into the family business. He offered to pay her more at J.E. Dunn than she could make as a medical technologist. Rosalie stuck with medical technology, working at St. Joseph's Hospital in Kansas City and years later at a doctor's office in Fort Lauderdale, Fla., after she was married.

The War Years

*I*t's a popular myth to think that the Japanese caught the United States totally unprepared for war when they bombed Pearl Harbor in 1941. Actually, the nation was gearing up its military machine for almost two years before it officially entered World War II. American shipyards, airplane manufacturers, and ammunition plants had already stepped up their production to meet the growing demand for weapons in

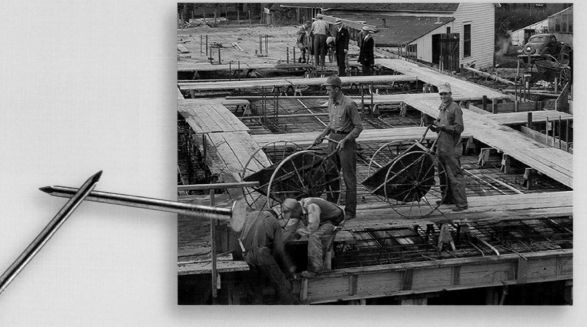

Before the concrete pump came along, workers had to rely on Georgia buggies like these, along with brute strength, to move concrete at a construction site.

Big advances were made in construction technology between the 1880s, when William T. Dunn, the carpenter, was helping build the Union Depot, and the 1920s, when his son, J.E. Dunn, began a building business. Construction took a big leap forward when the gas-powered engine that propelled the automobiles of Henry Ford was modified for use in large construction equipment such as bulldozers. The same work that would have required teams of horses in 19th century construction could be performed in a fraction of the time with the new technology. The steep slopes that were graded in a few weeks time on the Fairfax housing project during World War II would have taken months to grade fifty years earlier.

Despite the significant advances, construction technology of the first half of the 20th century was primitive by today's standards in many ways. Construction equipment now taken for granted, such as the concrete pump, simply didn't exist then. If a contractor needed a large amount of concrete moved from Point A to Point B in a short period of time, he lined up a crew of men and equipped them with oversized wheelbarrows called Georgia buggies.

Power tools were just a dream then; carpenters relied on elbow grease to push saws, hammer nails, and turn screws. The work was harder for hod carriers and masons who made mortar at the construction site; they would dip into large tanks of liquid lime to add to the mortar mixes when needed. Hod carriers depended upon brute strength to move loads of brick and mortar around a job. More often than not, manpower rather than machinery was the driving force behind any delivery system on a construction site.

Europe, where war had raged since 1939. The federal government had already hired private contractors such as J.E. Dunn to build housing for the defense workers in the war industry.

On the day of the Pearl Harbor attack, December 7, 1941, a photograph was taken on a bluff overlooking the Fairfax industrial district of Kansas City, Kan. It was a stark scene of dirt, leafless trees, and gray sky without a building in sight. Within days, J.E. Dunn began building a $1.5 million housing project on the 86-acre tract for the families of 350 workers at three defense plants in Fairfax: North American Aviation Inc., the Fruehauf Trailer Co., and the Aircraft Accessories Corp. Pictures taken later that month show one- and two-story wood frame houses filling the same view. Under young Ernie Jr.'s supervision, 40 of the 103 two-, four-, and six-family units were erected that December with the help of nearly 700 construction workers.

Controversies at the onset of the job had threatened its progress. First, the job's start was delayed during the fall of 1941. Seventeen homeowners whose houses had been cleared from the site complained that the government had not paid them in the condemnation proceedings. Once the issue was settled, subcontracted workers from Bowen

Construction immediately began grading the steep terrain in late November.

Then, days after the bulldozers began terracing the bluff, Senator Harry S. Truman of Missouri cited the Fairfax project as an example of government waste. Truman charged that taxpayers had to pay $3,000 an acre just to grade the site. Federal court appraisers Grant W. Harrington, C.A. Lowder, and Harry A. Smith disputed the Truman figure and said that grading only cost $409 an acre. The appraisers found the unit cost per family to be about $3,840 as compared to a similar project at Louisville, Ky., where the cost was $4,090. The Missouri senator who would one day be president was making a name for himself as a critic of government spending on the home front during the early war years, but he missed the mark when he aimed at the defense housing just west of his state line.

"Give 'Em Hell Harry" wasn't entirely wrong about the Fairfax project – the government probably could have saved a little extra money by cutting out some of the frills. Unlike the St. Louis and Denver public housing projects already undertaken by J.E. Dunn, the Fairfax project tried to give the living spaces a homey look. The exteriors were painted in varying shades of gray, red, and blue with doors and windows trimmed in white. Front porches

With the help of nearly 700 workers, J.E. Dunn built 40 multi-unit houses at the Fairfax war housing project in the weeks immediately following the Pearl Harbor attack.

were bordered in white latticework. The landscaping costs included planting 5,200 small trees and shrubs and plots were set aside for individual "victory" gardens. Much of the total $1.5 million budget also went toward the essentials: sewer, gas, and water mains had to be laid and roads built and paved for the newly built community. A few months into its construction, the housing project was named Quindaro Homes.

The local newspapers often quoted the builder during a large construction project. Ernie Sr. gave the *Kansas City Star* a historical view during the Fairfax project. "The government's far-sighted policy on defense housing will be a boon to the workers and eliminate much of the congestion experienced in big production centers in the First World War." He added, "I am glad to have had the opportunity to play a part in the defense effort." Ernie Sr.

would soon be playing an even larger role in the war effort and so would the job's superintendent, Ernie Jr.

Ernie Jr. became an enlisted man in the Navy's aviation cadet program in June 1942, a few weeks after families started moving into Quindaro Homes. He graduated from the Naval Air Station in Pensacola, Fla., that December, and chose to become a pilot in the Marine Air Corps. Once out of Pensacola, Ernie didn't have to wait long to test his flight skills in real battle across the Pacific Ocean. He landed on Midway Island just after the Americans had won a decisive victory there, and later flew into battle in the Marshall Islands. His plane took enemy fire during many sorties and his gunner was shot to death on one mission. He flew a total of 118 bombing missions in the Pacific and received several air medals.

A Patriot in War Time

*B*ack in Kansas City, Ernie Sr. showed his own unique and generous brand of patriotism on the construction company's next defense project, the Quartermaster Depot, located south of Hardesty and Independence avenues. Military engineers began asking questions about the bidding on the three Army warehouses because J.E. Dunn turned in a bid that was $250,000 less than next lowest contractor. "I don't

want to make any profit out of a war contract," Ernie Sr. told them in early 1942, "I'd like to build this at cost. All I want to do is keep my organization together so my sons can carry it on after the war."

The construction company had a few other jobs going on at the same time, but Ernie Sr. put his best superintendents, Amos Timms and Harry Gilchrist, in charge of the military warehouses. They shared the supervision of day and evening shifts of 300 workers. Future J.E. Dunn superintendents Woody Randolph and Charlie Bannister were carpenter foremen on the job, and Bill Dunn joined the labor crew that summer. "All summer long, three other laborers and I carried 4x4s on our shoulders to a sawmill at the site. My mother made a shoulder pad to help me carry the 4x4s that weighed about 75 pounds apiece," Bill said.

While Bill was toting lumber that summer, he probably stopped to get water once in a while from 14-year-old Thornton Cooke. "I was a water boy at the Quartermaster Depot, making 40 cents an hour," Thornton, now a retired insurance executive, remembers. His job was to walk the site with a bucket of water in each hand, a ladle in his pocket, and wait until the next laborer yelled, 'Hey water boy, get over here.' The Kansas City Health Department didn't approve of workers sharing a ladle from open buckets of water

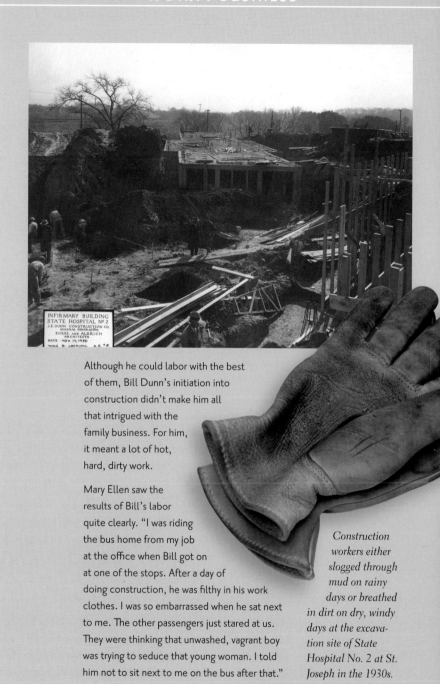

Although he could labor with the best of them, Bill Dunn's initiation into construction didn't make him all that intrigued with the family business. For him, it meant a lot of hot, hard, dirty work.

Mary Ellen saw the results of Bill's labor quite clearly. "I was riding the bus home from my job at the office when Bill got on at one of the stops. After a day of doing construction, he was filthy in his work clothes. I was so embarrassed when he sat next to me. The other passengers just stared at us. They were thinking that unwashed, vagrant boy was trying to seduce that young woman. I told him not to sit next to me on the bus after that."

Construction workers either slogged through mud on rainy days or breathed in dirt on dry, windy days at the excavation site of State Hospital No. 2 at St. Joseph in the 1930s.

Construction workers had to depend on wood scaffolding for support at the Quartermaster Depot.

Out of all his days on the job that summer of 1942, July 1 made the biggest impression on 14-year-old water boy Thornton Cooke, both literally and figuratively. That afternoon, 32,000 square feet of wooden scaffolding fell on him and 74 other workmen. The accident happened while workers were erecting concrete form work from the basement to the ground level. The *Kansas City Star* described the scene: "The framework was swarming with men when the collapse occurred, spilling scores of them into the basement of the structure in a tangle of lumber. Many were buried in the clattering debris."

"I was on the ground level of the building when a 4x4 grazed my neck and knocked me forward," Thornton remembers. "Then the biggest part of the scaffolding fell and brought more 4x4's down on my back." He dug his way out. Someone from the medical staff attached to the depot treated his cuts at the site. He fared better than at least 12 workers who were taken to nearby St. Mary's Hospital for injured backs, broken noses and fractures to their arms, legs, and ribs. For Thornton, the day wasn't a total loss: his name appeared in the newspaper that evening and he got to enjoy the stunned expressions of the other bus passengers when the shirtless teenager with the bandaged back stepped on board.

and made Thornton and the two other water boys switch to paper cups and closed water containers with spigots. "The workers didn't like the change to paper cups because they didn't hold as much water. They wanted the ladle back," said Cooke.

Though an accident with falling scaffolding interrupted work on July 1, no one was seriously injured, and the two-a-day work shifts resumed at the job within a week. Bill ended the summer the way he'd started it – lugging around 4x4s – before transferring to Notre Dame as a junior in the fall, where he enlisted in the Naval Reserve program to become a deck officer. His father had persuaded him to take civil engineering courses at Notre Dame, thinking Bill could apply his knowledge in the construction business, but the war intervened and put his father's career plans for him on hold. After attending Ernie Jr.'s graduation from the Naval Flight School in December 1942, Bill decided to become a military pilot too. Bill could have stayed in the Naval Reserve program at Notre Dame for his senior year but instead left the college at the end of his junior year to become a pilot in the Navy Air Corps.

In the spring of 1943, about the time that Bill was turning in his last exam at Notre Dame, the Quartermaster Depot project was finished a month ahead of

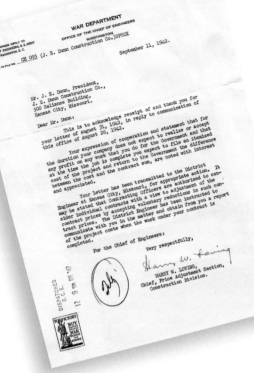

A letter from Harry W. Loving, one of the heads of the construction division at the U.S. War Department, thanks Ernie Dunn for giving up his profits on the Quartermaster Depot.

schedule. With the scaffolding accident old news by then, the newspaper headlines refocused in late May 1943: "Contractor Turns Back Profits on Army Depot" (Washington D.C. *Evening Star*), "Contractor Gives Back $400,000 To Government in War Profits" (*The Nashville Tennesseean*), "Rejects Profit On War" (*The New York Times*). The front page headline on the May 24 edition of the *Kansas City Star* simply read "Profits Back His Sons" with a subhead announcing, "Contractor Proves Patriotism by Giving Up $400,000."

When Ernie Sr. discovered he would make a profit of $178,000 on the depot – a job he intended to build for cost – Ernie asked the Army Engineers office to renegotiate the contract. He wanted his fee to be reduced by $150,000 on a contract that was already $250,000 less than any other bidder on the job. He said he would pay federal taxes with the remaining $28,000 and distribute the balance to the Red Cross, the USO, and other organizations. He wasn't looking for publicity, but when the war department insisted on telling the story, he agreed.

"I have two sons in the armed forces," Ernie Sr. told newspaper reporters. "I would feel it an empty victory if I lost one of them in winning this war. But I believe I would feel a lot worse if I made a lot of money out of the war and lost a son. It is my feeling that I am helping protect them by doing at cost whatever war work I do."[2]

Editorial writers across the country praised Ernie Sr. for his generosity toward the war effort. President Franklin D. Roosevelt recognized the magnitude of his contribution in a written letter. Almost 60 years later, in its Aug. 30, 1999 edition, *Engineering News-Record* included Ernie Sr. in its list of the top 125 people in the construction industry. The publication specifically cited his $400,000 donation during the war as one reason he made a list

that included Thomas Edison and Frank Lloyd Wright Jr.

Building More with Less

*B*ack in 1943, the heightened pace of construction work left Ernie Sr. little time to bask in the favorable publicity. Before the Quartermaster Depot was even completed, he'd started construction on a war housing project for the Sunflower Ordnance Plant southwest of De Soto, Kan. He beat out 18 other contractors to build 175 single-story residential buildings near the plant with a bid of $1,612,177. The buildings would house 852 families. One of the other contractors, the S. Patti Construction Co., outbid J.E. Dunn on the building of a grade school, a commercial building, and a community center at the site. Designed by the local city planner Hare & Hare in association with Marshall & Brown Architects and Engineers, the project would be the largest single housing development ever erected in the Kansas City area. The federal government wanted it to be a rush job just as the Fairfax and depot projects had been: Ernie was supposed to finish the housing within 90 days of breaking ground at the site. The construction schedule called for completion and occupancy of some of the buildings ahead of the others; ordnance workers and their families would move

Ernie Dunn in the 1930s.

When unions began organizing the building trades in the 1930s, they often met with resistance from management. Bill Dunn heard stories about some union representatives who came to a J.E. Dunn construction site during the Depression, asking to negotiate with Ray Bell, the superintendent. Bell said, "Fine, come around to my car." He opened the trunk, pulled out a shotgun and told them he was ready to negotiate.

Ernie Sr. took a more civilized approach toward the unions. Bill remembers that he was a teenager when his father and the head of the local carpenters union sat in lawn chairs on the Dunn's front lawn one summer night and negotiated the carpenters contract for the Kansas City area.

into the finished units, while construction workers continued building some of the others.

Minor delays to the schedule occurred: equipment didn't show up on time and the utility companies couldn't hook the housing project into their systems fast enough. A labor shortage threw another wrench into the works: there weren't enough brick and stonemasons available to erect the cinder-block walls of the buildings. Without masons to erect the walls, carpenters, painters, electricians, plumbers and other finishers couldn't begin their work. Eventually the labor crunch eased, the Sunflower families moved into their new quarters, and the construction delays failed to slow output at the ordnance plant.

The shortage of manpower experienced at the De Soto project wasn't unusual during World War II. The military's needs put everyday items such as nylon and different metals in short supply, too. Anticipating a metal shortage, Sunflower planners used substitutes where they could. Iceboxes in the apartment kitchens were made almost entirely of composition board instead of metal, sink cabinets were made of wood, and plastic was used for faucets and handles. Americans on the home front accepted the substitutes and adjusted to everyday inconveniences such as gas rationing –

Manpower wasn't a problem when the Fairfax housing project (left) was built at the outbreak of World War II, but it became one at the De Soto project (below), built in 1943.

grumbling and complaining would have sounded unpatriotic. J.E. Dunn took out a newspaper advertisement that expressed the prevailing sentiment, "No mere structural achievement, here in the safety of inland America, is worthy of comparison for a moment with the heroic acts of our brave men and women who are risking their lives on the field of battle."[3]

Ernie Sr. rephrased the patriotic message to an audience of the Builders' Association of Kansas City that had elected him their president in 1942:

"At this time when the very existence of our nation is at stake, we in the construction industry are in a position to render great service to our government.

We owe much to our government for the heritage that has been handed down to us for generations. So tonight, I would ask all, both management and labor, to pull together with one thought in mind, that we shall not fail in our duty to those who are laying down their lives in the service of their country."

After Ernie Sr. had already "rendered great service to our government" himself by turning down war profits and successfully constructing war housing, a governmental body made one more request of him. The U.S. Army offered to make him a brigadier general in its Corps of Engineers if he would oversee construction of Army barracks in Alaska, an area attacked by the Japanese along its Aleutian Islands chain. When Rose caught wind of the Army's offer to send her husband northward, she answered for him: "Absolutely not." He remained in Kansas City, free of battle wounds and frostbite. When his year term as president of the Builders' Association of Greater Kansas City was over, he became president of the Kansas City Chapter of the Associated General Contractors in 1943. And he continued backing the war effort. The U.S. Department of the Treasury recognized his help in raising money for several war bond drives and the United Seamen's Service attested to his support of its merchant seamen.

(above) Ernie Dunn Sr.(left) and Henry J. Mass-man Sr.(center) were made Knights of St. Gregory by Pope Pius XII. Bishop Edwin V. O'Hara (right), the Catholic bishop of Kansas City, conferred the honor on them in 1944.

(right) J.E. Dunn completed the retreat house for St. John's Seminary in Kansas City in 1942.

The Pope Takes Notice

*E*ven though the war effort and two builders' associations took up so much of his time, Ernie Sr. continued building for Catholic institutions during the war years. With several deadlines for government housing hanging over his head, Ernie Sr. completed a retreat house for St. John's Seminary at 72nd and Euclid in Kansas City in the spring of 1942. The two-story retreat house was designed by Joseph B. Shaughnessy, a Kansas City architect who had designed many Catholic churches in the area.

The following spring, J.E. Dunn workers returned to the newly built Bishop Lillis High School. Enrollment had grown so fast at the school since its opening a few years before that another floor of classrooms was already needed. Fresh out of Notre Dame and waiting to be called to active duty by the Navy Air Corps, Bill Dunn worked alongside other laborers on the high school rooftop. He was paid for building forms and pouring concrete during the day but didn't make any money for his nighttime job of timekeeping and doing payroll for the project. "Payroll had gotten more

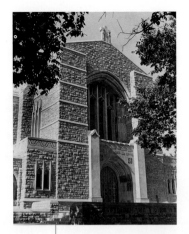

*J.E. Dunn began construction on
St. Peter's Church in 1944.*

complicated about that time when the government began requiring employers to take out withholding taxes," according to Bill. He soon took on another role at the Lillis addition – as a project troubleshooter. The superintendent, an older man, hadn't kept a close enough eye when the shoring around the support columns was erected. Later, when concrete for the new rooftop was being poured into column forms, Bill noticed the formwork start to move because the shoring below had not been properly braced. It was sheer luck that kept the shoring from collapsing. His father put the blame on the superintendent and replaced him with a man named Charlie Bannister, who would serve the company faithfully for many years.

Bill left the Lillis job that August after one of his former professors at Rockhurst College asked him to teach a course on celestial navigation to Army Air Corps cadets at the college. Bill had never taken a course on the subject but the professor kept him about a week ahead on the lesson plan. "The Army Air Corps students probably thought I was just a slacker, because they

didn't know that I was waiting to get my orders from the Navy Air Corps. I told them in September when the orders finally came through and got the raspberry from the class for being a Navy man."

With both sons in the service and the Lillis addition nearly completed, Ernie Sr. began another religious project. Joseph Shaughnessy, the architect he'd worked with on the retreat house at St. John's Seminary, introduced him to nuns from the Benedictine Sisters Convent of Perpetual Adoration in Clyde, Mo. Ernie Sr. helped the sisters in converting a large house at 4408 Rockhill Road in Kansas City into a temporary convent in the fall of 1943. The head of the convent, Mother Mary Dolorosa, wrote to Ernie, thanking him and telling him about the sisters' hope of later building a larger permanent convent on a hill off Meyer Boulevard. Ernie had told Mr. Shaughnessy about wanting Kansas City to have a religious shrine like the ones he had seen in the eastern United States and Canada. Mother Mary Dolorosa wrote that she too wanted such a shrine in Kansas City. Ernie would later help her realize that dream – but it would be several years after the war.

About the time that the war housing jobs were winding down, Ernie broke ground in February 1944 at St. Peter's

Church. It was located at Holmes Road and Meyer Boulevard, a few blocks west of where the Benedictine Sisters would eventually have their shrine. The St. Peter's job teamed him up again with Joseph Shaughnessy as chief architect. Carroll and Dean were associate architects on the project. The limestone, Gothic-styled church would win accolades for the architects after it was completed in the spring of 1946. The Kansas City chapter of the American Institute of Architects cited it as the most outstanding example of institutional architecture in the area for 1947. Few churches that would be designed in the postwar period would earn such praise – St. Peter's Church was one of the last of its kind in Kansas City. Tighter budgets, higher labor costs, and changing styles led postwar architects to design starker, more modern houses of worship whose exteriors sometimes were barely recognizable as churches.

All the work he'd done for Catholic institutions eventually brought a special honor to Ernie Sr. In September 1944, Bishop Edwin V. O'Hara, the Catholic bishop of Kansas City, told him and another Kansas City contractor, Henry J. Massman Sr., that Pope Pius XII had made them Knights of St. Gregory, one of the highest church honors that a layperson can be awarded. Mr. Massman was cited for his financial backing of Rockhurst College and other Catholic organizations. The college later named its administration building Massman Hall in his honor. Rockhurst College, the Sisters of Charity of Leavenworth, the Sisters of Mercy, the Benedictine Sisters, and other religious organizations had all benefited from Ernie Sr.'s work and support. Only one other Kansas Citian had ever received the award, Paul Froeschl, who was honored in 1942. Bishop O'Hara officially conferred the honor on the two contractors on Dec. 17, 1944, in the chapel at his residence at 5306 Sunset Drive. Lieutenant J. Ernest Dunn Jr. was in town to attend the investiture ceremony after serving in the South Pacific for sixteen months. Bill couldn't be there because he was in the same flight-training program in Pensacola that his older brother had graduated from two years before.

New Families and a New Era

W orld War II marked a turning point for the American family in many ways. Teenaged sons and brothers were expected to become servicemen almost overnight. Daughters and sisters became brides just as fast — and sometimes mothers

and sometimes widows not so long afterward. While the war continued, one thing remained constant in the Dunn family: the attention that Ernie Sr. and Rose gave to their children.

Despite his busy schedule, Ernie Sr. went to Notre Dame during the fall of 1943 to watch Bill play football in an intramural competition. More than a year later, he was at his younger son's bedside at the University of Iowa Medical Center — Bill had an emergency appendectomy shortly after landing a Navy light plane at a base in Iowa City. Overseas phone calls were expensive then, but Ernie Sr. and Rose talked to Ernie Jr. on the phone whenever he was in Hawaii.

If Ernie Sr. were vying for Father of the Year recognition, he'd at least have won

(above) Rosalie was in high school during most of World War II.

(left) Bill (left) and Ernie Jr. (right) were home on leave from the Navy when this picture was taken with their father.

(below left) Bill became a pilot in the Navy Air Corps during the war.

(below right) Ernie Sr. and his oldest daughter, Mary Ellen. With her father by her side, Mary Ellen took a train to San Diego to marry Roy Daly on March 3, 1945.

honorable mention when he saved Mary Ellen's wedding day. Mary Ellen had become engaged to Roy Daly, a senior lieutenant in the Navy, and they had set a wedding date for March 1945, when he was supposed to be on leave and could return to Kansas City. Mary Ellen had been working at the J.E. Dunn office as a bookkeeper up until this time. She had already hired a woman, Miss Bate, to take her place at the office when the word came that Roy's leave was cancelled; the Navy wouldn't let him leave the naval station in San Diego even for his own wedding. Ernie Sr. stepped in at this point, told Mary Ellen to pack her bags, he was going to take the train to California with her. "In those days there were so many military people riding the trains that you could barely get a ticket, but Dad knew a man at Union Station who got us two tickets. Dad and I rode westward for two-and-a-half days and Roy and I were married in California on March 3, 1945."

A few months later Ernie Jr. exchanged vows with Ann Trave, a Kansas City woman who'd graduated from St. Teresa's Academy, the same girls' high school where Mary Ellen and Rosalie had gone.

About the same time, Bill got his gold wings from Pensacola but didn't fly in combat. "I had my orders to report to the Battleship Wisconsin which was supposed to go out for the big push to Japan and then atomic bombs were dropped on Hiroshima and Nagasaki. The war ended and they didn't know what to do with us. I was transferred from the naval base at San Diego up to Alameda Naval Air Station, just outside of San Francisco. I flew there for three months and got away with murder – chasing the seals off the rocks, flying under the Golden Gate Bridge, a few things like that."

A new era was beginning for America and Ernie Sr. had anticipated it. He spoke of it in 1943 in his parting speech as president of the Builders' Association of Kansas City: "The construction industry and all forms of industry are soon coming to the crossroads, where plans of gigantic size must be made…. During the past few years, very little private construction work has been carried on so that after the war, a real sales campaign should be put forth for the construction of new factory buildings and municipal and state improvements such as schools, hospitals, roads, and bridges. [Our sons] have given up everything to go forth to all parts of the world to fight that you and I might enjoy the blessings of this grand country. When peace is made…it is our obligation to see that these boys again have the opportunity to carry on where they left off. We must guarantee that they have not lost at home what they went to fight for in foreign lands." The challenge for his construction company after the war was implementing some of those "plans of gigantic size" – erecting housing, schools, and other construction fast enough to meet the needs of the returning war veterans and their growing families.

J.E. Dunn announces its support for the war effort with an advertisement in the Kansas City Star newspaper.

The Motherhouse of the Sisters of Charity in Leavenworth was built by J.E. Dunn before World War II. The construction company returned nearly 60 years later, renovating and making additions to the property.

Chapter 2
BRICK BY BRICK
1945-1964

The Benedictine Convent of Perpetual Adoration,
south of the intersection of Meyer Boulevard and
the Paseo in Kansas City, Mo.

POSTWAR YEARS

The Homecoming

AMERICAN SOLDIERS WHO SUR-
VIVED WORLD WAR II RETURNED
TO A HOMELAND THAT WAS UN-
PREPARED TO MEET ONE OF THEIR
BASIC NEEDS: HOUSING. ERNIE
PREDICTED THAT NEED. HE BEGAN
CONSTRUCTION ON THE VICTORY
COURT APARTMENTS IN KANSAS
CITY'S COUNTRY CLUB PLAZA
DISTRICT IN OCTOBER 1944, IN-
TENDING TO RENT IT OUT TO THE
WAR VETERANS, THEIR FAMILIES,
AND THE FAMILIES OF WORKERS
IN THE DEFENSE INDUSTRY. WHEN
THE WAR ENDED, HE WAS STILL
ASSISTING THE FEDERAL GOVERN-
MENT IN PROVIDING HOUSING, BUT
INSTEAD OF BUILDING RESIDENCES

Ernie Jr. set up an office in this building on Holmes, north of 27th Street, while supervising veterans' housing projects after World War II.

FOR WAR INDUSTRY WORKERS
AS HE HAD ON THE SUNFLOWER
VILLAGE AND QUINDARO HOMES
PROJECTS, HIS POSTWAR EFFORTS
FOR THE FEDERAL HOUSING
AUTHORITY WERE MEANT TO HELP
RETURNING VETERANS.

*T*he veterans' emergency housing
projects were comparable in size to
the federal housing jobs Ernie built during
the war and their schedules were just as
tight. For one federal contract, J.E. Dunn
Construction Company had to dismantle
houses and Army barracks in surrounding
states and move them to Penn Valley
Park in Kansas City, where they would
temporarily house veterans and their
families. Other contractors were involved

Bill dons cap and gown for his 1946 graduation at Rockhurst College.

in constructing sidewalks and roadways and installing utility connections for the recycled units. Ernie Jr., a returning war veteran himself, stepped back into an executive role for J.E. Dunn Construction, supervising several of the veterans' housing projects. His father hoped to find a management position in the company for Ernie Jr.'s younger brother, but Bill had more pressing things on his mind, namely his upcoming wedding, in February of 1947, to Jean Aylward.

In the meantime, Bill scrambled to finish his college degree. "I think I took 31 hours the spring semester of 1946 at Rockhurst College, and graduated with bachelor's degrees in mathematics and physics that August." Bill wanted to

interview for a position at the newly founded Midwest Research Institute in Kansas City; several key people at the research institute had close ties with Bill's professors at Rockhurst. At this point, however, Ernie Sr. intervened.

"You've never seen the business side of the construction business," his father told Bill. "Do me a favor and just give it a try." Ernie Sr. sent his younger son to Hannibal, Mo., where the construction company was using materials from dismantled Army houses to build housing for veterans.

"It was an interesting assignment but the wages were ridiculously low," Bill remembers. He was paid $50 a week, but received no reimbursement for the bus fare to and from Hannibal and had to pay for his own meals and lodging at the Mark Twain Hotel in Hannibal. He brought the work records into Kansas City every weekend and worked half the day on Saturdays, giving his reports. "I was the payroll and material clerk and learning construction at the same time," Bill remembers. "It would usually end up that I had about ten dollars left over for a date

on the weekend." Bill never did interview for the job at Midwest Research Institute, however. When the Hannibal job wrapped up in 1947, Bill took his next J.E. Dunn assignment in Kansas City, and continues working for the company to this day.

Bill looks back on his first years at J.E. Dunn Construction Company. "When I started, the company had a net worth of about $400,000. Our main office was still on the top floor of the Reliance Building, a five-story building at 10th and McGee. The building has since been razed and the last addition to the Federal Reserve Bank is now at that location. There were only three other people at the office besides my father and me. In 1947, my brother was working out of another office for the company, managing war housing projects. It was a whole different arrangement then as far as operations went. There were three or four main superintendents, and usually a superintendent in those days was the meanest, toughest person who could whip anyone on the job. I don't think any of the superintendents had been to college. A few of them may have gone to high school, but I wouldn't even bet on that." The next generation of superintendents, however, would prove to be as smart as they were tough.

Jean Aylward was an attractive woman, and a few other servicemen had already popped the question to her before Bill half-jokingly proposed marriage at a mutual friend's party on Thanksgiving Day, 1945. After several months of dating and a few more serious proposals from her tenacious suitor, Jean finally said "yes."

Bill likes to tell people that the proposal happened one summer day at the Dunn's swimming pool in Stanley, Kan. Bill's mother and Jean's mother were both poolside, Bill was in the pool, and Jean dove into the water, wearing her new two-piece swimming suit. When she surfaced topless, her mother shrieked, "Jean!"

"I asked her to marry me right then and there," Bill says. Actually, the proposal took place at an even more unlikely spot: the downstairs vault at Columbia National Bank, where Jean was working.

(left) Jean Aylward and Bill Dunn sit in front of a diner on Wornall Road.

(top) Jean and Bill, 1946.

(right) Wedding Day, February 15, 1947.

A Cohort of
Hardworking Men

$\mathcal{E}$rnie Jr. and Bill were just two of many World War II veterans who would guide the company through some of its most important years. Another vet, Jack McCollom, was regarded as one of the shrewdest general superintendents ever to work for the construction company. He had seen a lot of action on board a battleship, where he handled damage control. Bill remembers how Jack's war experiences helped him manage a grim assignment late in his career: the cleanup effort at the Hyatt Regency Hotel in Kansas City after its skywalk collapsed in 1981, killing scores of people.

Another war veteran, Dick Neumann, began working as a bricklayer's apprentice for J.E. Dunn in December 1945. Japanese warplanes had bombed the Navy ship he served on during the war and killed many of his shipmates. If the war left any mental scars, none of the people he worked with at J.E. Dunn for 50 years saw them manifested. Dick rose in the ranks at the construction company, becoming that rarity among operations people: the even-tempered superintendent. He worked his crews as hard as other J.E. Dunn superintendents, but the consensus is that he may have been the nicest, most well-liked person ever to reach that position in the company. Where superintendents of the past resembled tyrants who used heavy-handed threats and coercion to push jobs along, Dick was more like a coach who could drive his workers when needed, but preferred to inspire them with a sense of teamwork.

Rafford Davis, a World War II vet and an African-American, knew something about the importance of endurance before he ever put on a military uniform. During the war, he served in a racially segregated Army troop in Alaska's Aleutian Islands, the same area where the Army Corps of Engineers had asked Ernie Sr. to direct the construction of Army barracks. Rafford cooked for his troops during the war and received an offer from one of the other soldiers to open a diner with him in California after the war. Instead, Rafford got married to a midwestern woman and settled in Kansas City, where her relatives lived. Rafford began working for a construction company where worker safety was low on the list of priorities. After barely escaping serious injury on one of that contractor's jobs, Rafford went to work for J.E. Dunn in the late 1940s and soon was impressing foremen with his productivity. Promotions for black workers were rare in the construction industry then, but Rafford was promoted to superintendent of J.E. Dunn's cement finishers when he demonstrated how he could pour and spread concrete twice as fast as any other worker. When asked if it was hard to get white laborers to take orders, Rafford says, "No, because I never asked them to do work that I wouldn't do myself."

Despite the odds, he defused the race issue with his own hard work. On weekends when he wasn't working for J.E. Dunn, Rafford moonlighted by pouring concrete driveways and sidewalks at people's homes.

Viewing war films such as the Academy Award-winning *Saving Private Ryan* is as close as most Americans can come to experiencing the Allied invasion on D-Day, the turning point in World War II. Another former J.E. Dunn superintendent, John Spencer, lived the experience as an Army paratrooper, dropping behind enemy lines in Normandy. "Tough," "shrewd," and "intelligent" – traits that made him a good soldier – are the words J.E. Dunn employees used to characterize John. Like his future employer, Bill Dunn, John was in college at the outbreak of World War II. He was a freshman at the University of Kansas studying to be an engineer and working summers as a carpenter's apprentice before the war interrupted his life. Though he didn't return to college after the war, he never lost his disciplined study habits. When he became a carpenter foreman and then a superintendent for J.E. Dunn, he would take his work home with him, studying the blueprints and devising ways to expedite the work on a project.

Rafford Davis served in the Army during World War II.

John, the driven student, was known as an intense teacher to the many J.E. Dunn employees who worked for him. His lessons were often bitter pills to swallow – John didn't worry much about sparing an employee's feelings – but his lessons were rarely forgotten.

A lesson that many World War II vets learned all too well during the war years was how frail life could be. Bill Miller knew that just as a bullet could snuff out one's life in a second's time, death could strike just as swiftly at a construction site.

On the very first job for which hardhats were required, the construction of Central Missouri State College in Warrensburg, one of those hardhats saved the life of a carpenter when a brick nearly shattered the headgear but spared the man's skull. After that incident, Bill kept the crushed hardhat in a clear plastic case near the entrance of his work trailer as a reminder of the importance of workplace safety. Bill, who collected war memorabilia and even opened a historical museum in his hometown of Pleasant Hill, Mo., stressed the importance of safety in the workplace before it was even popular.

Many other World War II vets who came to work for Dunn in the 1940s through the 1960s would make a lasting impact on the company: men such as

Charlie Wakeman, one of the company's first general superintendents, and Gene Payne, a former Marine, who was a timekeeper for the company before he became a project manager. Television commentator and writer Tom Brokaw has called the World War II veterans "The Greatest Generation" for their contribution to the United States during the war and throughout their lives. It's not too much of a stretch to call the group of men who came to work for the construction company after the war J.E. Dunn's greatest generation. They were the generation who embraced the values Ernie Sr. prized – a solid work ethic, fairness, and helping the less fortunate – and passed them on to the employees they mentored. They were the bridge between Ernie Sr. and the current generation of J.E. Dunn employees, people who would never know their company's founder.

Boom Times

*H*igh-minded values such as fairness and philanthropy weren't the first things the young veterans had on their minds when they returned home from the war. Mostly, they wanted to marry their sweethearts, have children, and get jobs that would let them support their new

families. For the construction industry, this meant the pace of business remained every bit as hectic as it had been during the war years. Instead of munitions plants and war housing, the needs now were for houses, hospitals, schools, churches, and new roadways for returning veterans and their growing families.

Contractors couldn't build fast enough to meet the demand, and shortages of building materials often delayed construction on their projects. J.E. Dunn began building three apartment buildings at 48th and Belleview in December 1945, but material shortages delayed the job for six months in 1946. The combination of high demand and limited supplies caused construction costs to edge upward, but for years demand held strong. As late as 1948, there was a waiting list of 3,500 veterans trying to get their families moved into barracks-type emergency housing in the Kansas City area. Only a few years later, as the children of veterans reached school age, a new building demand would be created for schools as well as hospitals and places of worship.

A writer for the *Kansas City Star* put some of the blame for the housing shortage on government agencies and the local citizenry: "We go back to 1945 to show that the war left us with scant appreciation of rental housing needs.

Now it is 1949 and, seemingly, we don't appreciate that rental housing still is this city's No. 1 physical need."[4] The writer cited the city planning commission's denial of Ernie Dunn's 1945 request to build a Georgian-styled apartment/hotel complex in the Brookside area; he called it an example of local indifference to the plight of renters. The Brookside complex would have been the largest piece of property owned by Ernie Sr., with 350 living units, but the city planning commission sided with more than 200 Brookside homeowners opposed to the development and turned him down. Prospective tenants would have to look elsewhere for their residences, to the newly incorporated suburbs.

Opportunities in a Growing City

*W*hen the city spread outward, the old streetcar lines fell from favor, replaced by the automobile. As the stream of automobile commuters to Kansas City's downtown increased, so did the need for available parking. One of the more successful downtown developers, Joseph A. Bruening, hired his brother-in-law, Ernie Dunn Sr., to build a four-story parking garage at 10th and Central in late 1945. Its 766 parking

J.E. Dunn built the Centennial Building (top) in 1950, on top of the Board of Trade Garage (below), an earlier J.E. Dunn project.

spaces were intended primarily for tenants in three of his properties: the Board of Trade, the Dwight Building, and the Insurance Exchange.

Bruening didn't believe in scrimping on style or quality. His architect on the project, Frank E. Trask, designed the outside of the structure with a streamlined version of the art deco style in mind. The inside was an example of "engineered parking," according to Bruening. "Each space has been worked out to provide maximum room and convenience," he told reporters. Before Ernie's company completed the four stories, his brother-in-law decided to add two more stories to make room for 1,200 vehicles. The structure eventually became known as the Board of Trade Garage.

Rose Dunn (far right) with her siblings (L-R): Marie Zahner, Henry Bruening, Leo Bruening, and Joe Bruening. Joe hired his brother-in-law, Ernie Dunn, to build several projects including Board of Trade Garage and the Centennial Building in downtown Kansas City.

Bruening must have liked the construction company's work. Less than five years later he selected J.E. Dunn to top off the parking garage with four stories of office space. Bruening named his new office space the Centennial Building, partly because of its location at 10th and Central and also to mark the occasion of Kansas City's 100th anniversary that year, 1950.

The favorable working relationship between Joe and Ernie Sr. probably helped strengthen the bond between two brothers-in-law who otherwise had little in common. Compared to his more modest brother-in-law, Joe Bruening liked the good life and didn't mind flaunting it. He and his wife, Della, lived in a colonial-style mansion that would have looked more in place on a southern plantation than outside of Liberty, Mo. He kept a small fleet of Lincoln Continental cars for personal use in an oversized garage on his estate and would send them to Texas to have air conditioning installed at a time when many people had never even heard of an air-conditioned car. Once, Joe tagged along with Rose and Ernie on a jaunt to Cuba during its wilder, pre-Castro days. His wife stayed home because she didn't like to fly in airplanes. During the trip, Joe burst into the Dunn's hotel room with an armload of cash to announce that he'd won enough money at the casinos to pay the traveling expenses for all three of them. Ernie became Joe's closest friend in later years and regularly accompanied him to the doctor's office when his health was failing.

Friendship and a good working relationship also helped Ernie Sr. land another job in 1945: building new offices for Columbia National Bank at 921 Walnut. J.E. Dunn Construction Company had proven itself to be a dependable customer at the bank during difficult financial times and Ernie Sr. had found a good friend in Charlie Aylward, the bank's senior vice president. There was an easy affinity between the two men. Both were sons of Irish immigrant parents and had grown up street smart in working class neighborhoods in Kansas City. Ernie Sr. and Charlie shared a few of the stereotypical traits of the Irish – a quick temper, a gift for gab, and a sense of humor – but both were conservative in their drinking and spending habits. They shared grandchildren in the coming years, too, after Ernie's son, Bill, married Charlie's daughter, Jean. On June 13, 1945, long before he could predict his daughter would be changing her name to Dunn, Charlie Aylward was one among several bank officers signing a resolution that applauded Mr. J.E. Dunn for finishing their building "with an expedition, completeness, and success most remarkable in wartime."

Commercial and industrial jobs would remain the toughest markets for J.E. Dunn to break into long after the garage and bank were built. Getting these jobs often depended upon luck, circumstance, and knowing the right people. For example, J.E. Dunn was able to negotiate work for the Hinde & Dauch Company at its corrugated box factory in Kansas City, Kansas, largely because the factory's plant manager, Willis Bannister, was a cousin of Charlie Bannister, a J.E. Dunn superintendent. Ernie Sr.'s membership on the Columbia National Bank's board of directors led him to another construction job in Kansas City, Kansas: Helmers Manufacturing, whose president happened to have a seat on the same bank board. J.E. Dunn got a third job in Kansas City, Kan., the old-fashioned way: it competitively outbid several other contractors to do work at the Colgate Palmolive Peet plant. For the most part, however, J.E. Dunn continued to depend on government and Catholic-sponsored jobs for much of its work well into the 1950s.

Hinde & Dauch plant.

Social Divisions

*T*he war may have shaken up a few institutions on the nation's social front, but there were some things in Kansas City that hadn't changed: Kansas Citians were still divided along racial and religious lines. Columbia National Bank, Ernie's bank, was unofficially known as the "Catholic" bank, and Thomas McGee & Sons, the insurance company that

helped him get his bonding, was one of the "Catholic" insurance agencies at the time. Catholics weren't often accepted into certain country clubs; the situation was worse for Jews and blacks who were explicitly barred from living in some area suburbs. Sometimes being Catholic was enough to prevent a contractor from getting a job. Bill remembers a time in 1948 when J.E. Dunn submitted the lowest bid for construction of the Ambulance Exchange Building located next to St. Mary's Hospital. J.E. Dunn lost the job when the architect, who belonged to a

Masonic lodge, said he would lower his fee if the owner would award the job to the next lowest bidding contractor, a fellow Mason. What angered Ernie Sr. most about the situation was that the owner who agreed to the architect's questionable terms was a Catholic himself. There was a flip side to discriminatory practices in the local construction industry, however – the Catholic dioceses in Missouri and Kansas weren't giving much of their work to non-Catholics at the time either.

Fortunately for J.E. Dunn, the government and Catholic-funded jobs

were plentiful after the war, so there was no shortage of work. A large part of its institutional work came from hospital expansions. Bill managed his first large-scale project on a five-story addition to St. Mary's Hospital at 28th and Main. The new hospital wing, completed in 1950, added 112 beds and new administrative and surgical quarters.

The same year, hospital construction peaked in the Kansas City area. An article in the *Kansas City Star* noted that about $20 million went to new hospitals and additions that year, increasing the area's hospital bed capacity from 4,800 to 6,000. J.E. Dunn contributed to that number by making the University of Kansas Medical Center – the area's largest hospital – even bigger.

Out-of-state communities were also expanding their hospital services at the time. With Bill as the project manager, J.E. Dunn started work on a $1 million hospital and clinic expansion at the College of Osteopathy and Surgery in Kirksville, Mo., in September 1949. Bill remembers the time well. His son, Bill Jr., was celebrating his first birthday while Jean was pregnant with their second son, Terrence Patrick, who was born October 14. All of Bill's siblings were either married or engaged by this time. His youngest sister, Rosalie, the last to wed, married Army Air Corps veteran Mike Donahue in 1950.

The business relationship J.E. Dunn developed with the Federal Housing Authority before World War II continued, but with different people in charge at the FHA after the war. As a Missouri senator in 1941, Harry Truman had initially criticized building costs at Quindaro Homes, one of J.E. Dunn's federal housing projects. As president in the late 1940s, Truman sought the construction company's help in bringing FHA housing to his hometown of Independence. Vivian Truman, Harry's brother and head of the FHA, telephoned Ernie Sr. after the construction company submitted a bid on an apartment complex, but the developer didn't have enough money to begin construction. Vivian told him that Harry wanted the apartment complex finished before he left office and asked Ernie Sr. to become both its developer and its contractor. Ernie agreed and assigned Bill as project manager and Jack McCollom as superintendent. "I hope you two know what you're doing," Ernie told his son and McCollom. The project turned out to be a success and the Liberty Manor Apartments became the first apartment complex in Independence built under the auspices of the Federal Housing Authority.

J.E. Dunn had proven its mettle with the U.S. military during World War II when it built the Quartermaster Depot at a breakneck pace. The company would prove itself again in the postwar period by building an armory for the Army Reserve Corps. The armory was one of 21 new structures being erected in 20 states as part of the reserve corps' expansion program. When J.E. Dunn first bid the job, it was supposed to be built on Signboard Hill, where the Westin Crown Center Hotel stands today, but the military couldn't get all the property owners to agree to the sales terms. An alternate site for the armory was found between 15th and 16th streets on Central Avenue, but the new site required new contract terms between the military and its contractors. Bill Dunn and Abe Jacobson of A.D. Jacobson, the mechanical contractor on the job, went to Omaha, Neb., where they negotiated new terms with the military over a two-day period. Construction began on August 15, 1950. Though the outbreak of the Korean conflict heightened pressure to finish the project on time, J.E. Dunn didn't give the military any reason to complain. With Woody Randolph as general superintendent, the construction company completed the armory and an adjoining warehouse on schedule.

Bill Dunn managed his first large-scale project on a five story addition to St. Mary's Hospital.

A Brief Adventure in Heavy Construction

*A*bout this same time, J.E. Dunn ventured into a totally new market for the company: heavy construction. Six or seven heavy contractors dominated the road construction market in Kansas City during the 1940s and 1950s. Ernie Jr. must have shocked them all when he submitted a $650,000 bid to the Missouri Department of Transportation for building the substructure for the Southwest Trafficway Viaduct – it was $200,000 less than the next lowest bid. Bill remembers how distressed his father, Ernie Sr., became when he learned about the low bid. "My sons are taking this company down the drain," their father shouted.

His oldest son allayed those fears when the project turned out to be quite profitable. Ernie Jr. kept the job ahead of schedule by using methods normally reserved for the construction of buildings. According to the December 1949 issue of *Contractors and Engineers Monthly*, an "assembly line" method of operation, use of tubular steel building scaffold as support for the heavy concrete viaduct beams, and prefabrication of steel reinforcing on the ground were some of the tactics he used to move the project along. The six-lane wide, half-mile-long viaduct took almost

(above) The six-lane, half-mile-long Southwest Trafficway Viaduct as a work in progress.

(left) The completed trafficway, November 1950.

two years to complete. At the ribbon cutting ceremony on November 16, 1950, Mayor William A. Kemp described the trafficway as "the most ultra-modern in urban highways."

The next road and bridge project for the company would prove to be its last. J.E. Dunn Construction was hired to construct the Baltimore Bridge to help connect the Plaza shopping district to areas south of Brush Creek. Problems in the quality of the concrete required that sections of the bridge be torn out and rebuilt a second time, and J.E. Dunn's profit margin suffered. In addition, J.E. Dunn bid on a job to do extra work on the Southwest Trafficway. The winning bid was equal to what would

have been J.E. Dunn's building cost. Ernie Sr. and company looked elsewhere for work after that experience.

The Prayer House on the Hilltop

*T*he postwar era was a busy period in Ernie Sr.'s life. When he wasn't overseeing a construction project he was looking after one of his growing number of real estate properties. Despite the crammed schedule, Ernie didn't forget the pledge he had made during the war to help the Benedictine Sisters of Perpetual Adoration build a religious shrine in Kansas City.

Near the end of the war, the nuns acquired the site they had hoped for: a prominent hill south of the intersection of the Paseo and Meyer boulevards. The sisters explained why the seven-acre tract was an ideal setting: "As soon as we saw this site, set apart, yet in the midst of the hurry and bustle of persons for whom we pray, we realized it would be a most fitting location."

Building a convent and chapel for the nuns became a special mission for Ernie Sr. and he agreed to do the work at cost. Joseph Shaughnessy, the man who first introduced Ernie to the nuns, was the shrine's architect. Ernie had already converted a house at 4408 Rockhill Road into a temporary convent for the sisters during the war, but its chapel could only seat fifty people and had gotten too crowded for the groups of lay people from 35 parishes who often stopped by to pray. The chapel proposed for the new site would seat 400. The new convent would also give the sisters more room for living quarters and for their work of sewing vestments and baking altar breads.

The Most Rev. Edwin V. O'Hara, the Catholic bishop of Kansas City, presided at the groundbreaking ceremony on Oct. 13, 1945. He would return more than three years later to seal the cornerstone at the shrine and declare: "The gates of this temple of hope will be open day and night for all men to enter for rest and meditation. It will be a retreat from the humdrum of everyday life where men can, through meditation, gain renewed strength and hope."[5]

Between the groundbreaking and the dedication, the construction project encountered a few challenges. Early on in the job, for example, one of the sisters complained about pinup posters at the project job office. The pictures quickly came down, the construction crews watched their language, and several workers even volunteered time at the job on Saturdays. An engineers' strike caused delays during the project's second year. Like many other construction jobs of the period, the shrine was plagued with material shortages and tardy deliveries.

When the convent and sanctuary finally began to take shape, people took notice. A writer for the *Kansas City Star* called the building "one of the most distinctive architectural additions to Kansas City in recent years. Early morning light gives a chaste white tone to the buff brick walls."[6] A writer for the order said the building's Adoration Chapel had characteristics of the Italian Renaissance and the Lombardic styles of architecture. Ernie Sr. gave the chapel a finishing touch when he anonymously donated

(top) Ernie Dunn Sr. donated four brass bells to the Benedictine Sisters Chapel.

(bottom) J.E. Dunn crews built a full-scale replica of the first Catholic church in Kansas City on the north lawn of the Benedictine Sisters Convent.

four brass bells to hang in its 100-foot tower. Ranging in size from 450 to 2,100 pounds, the bells rang for the first time at the dedication of the chapel on May 17, 1949. The bells weren't Ernie's only gifts for the shrine – he had already waived

1949 photo of the new J.E. Dunn office at 10th and Holmes.

J.E. Dunn has been its own best customer, periodically adding onto its headquarters on Holmes Street.

In the mid-1970s, an addition on the north side of the building more than doubled the size of office space. After the warehouse operations were moved to a site at 29th and Cherry Streets, the old warehouse space on the building's east side was converted to office space.

In 1995, the company added a 24,000 square foot expansion designed by the BNIM architectural firm for a new east wing. The building J.E. Dunn had leased to Brinks for more than 40 years was incorporated into the addition.

The 1995 addition nearly tripled the J.E. Dunn office space, but even more space was needed when the number of office employees exceeded 300 during the late 1990s. At the same time, the warehouse space on Cherry Street was getting more crowded with machinery and materials. The construction company bought the Safety Council Building at 901 Charlotte, across the street from its own offices, and, after a $4 million renovation and addition, opened it as additional J. E. Dunn office space in 2001. The warehouse space also expanded in 2001, when J.E. Dunn sold its Cherry Street property and moved the warehouse operations into a larger building on a 5-acre tract in North Kansas City. In 2002, the construction company bought a building for storing tarps, trailers, and scaffolding on Bell Street near Southwest Trafficway in Kansas City.

the construction fee and anonymously donated $10,000 to the project – and they wouldn't be his last.

Ernie Sr. pitched in again when an unusual request was asked of him in the spring of 1950. In June, while Kansas Citians were celebrating the city's centennial with historic pageants at Starlight Theatre and fireworks displays, Catholic leaders chose the occasion to observe 100 years of diocesan growth with a candlelit procession from nearby Bishop Hogan High School to the Benedictine Adoration Chapel. Ernie agreed to build a full-scale replica of the first Catholic church in Kansas City – a 30x20 ft. log building that once stood at 11th Street and Pennsylvania Avenue – close to where the Cathedral of the Immaculate Conception stands today. The construction company erected the replica on a terrace in front of the Perpetual Adoration Chapel just for the occasion and returned to dismantle it a few weeks after the nighttime procession.

In their new chapel, the Benedictine sisters continued their tradition of praying day and night in 30-minute relays. Each nun always began with the prayer, "I kneel in the divine presence in the name of all

men of all times of all countries, now and forever." During 1950, less than five years after the end of World War II, American soldiers fighting on foreign soil probably ranked high on the sisters' prayer lists. Today, more than fifty years later, the nuns have long since moved from the convent. "The Benedictine Convent of Perpetual Adoration was probably one of the construction projects closest to my dad's heart," Bill Dunn remembers. "It might sadden him to know that while sons and daughters still go to war, the Benedictine nuns don't pray at the shrine today."

A New Address for J.E. Dunn Construction Company

*I*n 1949, a year before the Kansas City centennial, J.E. Dunn marked its own milestone: a quarter century in the construction business. For much of the first 25 years, Ernie Sr. conducted business from offices rented on the fifth floor of the Reliance Building at 10th and McGee, but the space was starting to feel a little cramped for the growing company. "My brother had been working out of another location while he was managing several emergency war housing jobs. It became apparent that we'd need additional office space once he finished that work," Bill says. His father decided to build the new office in a blighted section of town at the northeast corner of 10th and Holmes. Why did he choose this less than ideal location? "Because it was cheap," Bill suggests. "My father bought the lot in a land clearance sale."

Ernie Sr. built a 7,000 square foot brick building on the site. Ernie Sr., his sons, and two secretaries – Miss Bate and Miss Mathews – used 2,000 square feet of the building for office space; the rest was used as a warehouse that abutted the company's materials yard. The company headquarters has remained at this location ever since, but the office space has changed dramatically in size and appearance over the years.

Not long after moving to the new address, Ernie Sr. constructed a one-story brick building just east of his offices. J.E. Dunn leased it to Brinks Inc. for a low rental fee. "He thought that having the armored car service company as a neighbor would make the area a safer place," Bill remembers.

Early photos of the J.E. Dunn office show a three-story brick apartment/hotel building – a flophouse, in fact – looming just to the north of the original office. The construction company razed it after buying the lot and tore down tenement buildings located west, north, and east of the original

site. J.E. Dunn used the new space for office expansions and more parking space. The rows of windows that once appeared along the 10th street and Holmes Avenue sides of the original J.E. Dunn office are gone now, bricked up after rioters began burning and looting in nearby neighborhoods in the late 1960s.

The 1950s: A Decade of Real Estate Ventures

Not many years after he had moved the company headquarters to 929 Holmes, Ernie Sr. began handing over the construction side of the business to his sons so he could devote more time to developing and managing real estate. He scored a number of real estate successes at this time, especially on apartments he had developed around the Plaza area. One very profitable transaction occurred in the 1950s, when he bought lots just north of the Plaza in exchange for the hotels on Euclid and Bellefontaine he had owned since the late 1920s. Though the $1.25 million, 10-story Dunleith Tower apartment building that J.E. Dunn built on the Plaza site during 1952 and 1953 – as well as two more nearly identical ones constructed a few years later – would never win awards for their architects, they

were very popular because of their prime location. The three reinforced concrete buildings finished in brick had very little charm, but they stood atop a hill just north of an upscale shopping district. Ernie Sr. and his wife, Rose, liked the location at 46th and Jefferson Street so well that they sold their house near Loose Park and moved into the penthouse suite of the original building in 1954. Ernie and Rose's young grandchildren loved to be there on December nights to gaze down on the Plaza Christmas lights. While Grandma played carols at the baby grand piano, Grandpa would slip them some candy.

Not all of Ernie Sr.'s real estate ventures struck gold the way the Dunleith Towers had; sometimes zoning boards turned his plans down flat. The city of Leavenworth, Kan., nixed his proposal to build a hotel in its downtown area. Brookside homeowners killed his plans for a hotel-apartment complex in their neighborhood. He tried teaming up with his brother-in-law, Joe Bruening, to develop a $20 million commercial and residential center in North Kansas City, but the plan was never executed. On other real estate ventures, Ernie Sr. often ignored the importance of location, and property values suffered in the long-term. The Swope Parkway shopping

An artist's rendering of the three Dunleith Towers.

J.E. Dunn added a three-story addition to Providence Hospital in Kansas City, Kan., in the late 1950s.

center, for example, built for $750,000 in 1959, would look abandoned less than 15 years later as the neighborhood became poorer, the crime rates soared, and tenants such as the A&P grocery moved their businesses elsewhere.

All the real estate ventures – the good ones as well as the bad ones – put demands on Ernie Sr.'s time. "My dad spent a large part of the day at offices he had on the Plaza where he managed many real estate holdings," Bill remembers. "He had about a thousand apartments in the Kansas City area. This would have included Independence, a number of them on the Plaza and in the central city. He would come down to our downtown office for maybe an hour or an hour-and-a half each day just to see what was going on. But for the last six years of his life, he wasn't really active in the construction business. It was principally run by my brother and myself." Ernie Sr.'s sons-in-law, Roy Daly and Mike Donahue, helped him manage the real estate.

The volume of construction work didn't suffer in Ernie Sr.'s absence, in part because his own real estate developments generated a fair amount of the construction work. In addition to the Dunleith holdings, Ernie Sr. grew his real estate holdings on the east side of Kansas City, building Paseo Court, which was 21 duplexes at 75th Street and the Paseo, and Swope Crestview, a 60-unit garden-type apartment complex directly south of Swope Parkway shopping center.

More Hospitals and Schools

*W*ork coming from J.E. Dunn's traditional client bases stayed strong. Older hospitals continued to expand their facilities throughout the 1950s. J.E. Dunn submitted a low bid for building a psychiatric receiving center at General Hospital, one of the construction company's customers before the war. The psychiatric center was scheduled to be built atop fill dirt, an unstable site upon which to erect a building. For better column support, J.E. Dunn used drilled piers for the first time, drilling down an extra 25 feet to attach the building into firmer bedrock. In 1953, the company built Stormont-Vail Hospital in Topeka, using drilled piers once again.

Less than five years after it had completed expansions to St. Mary's Hospital and the University of Kansas Medical Center in the early 1950s, J.E. Dunn returned to make more substantial additions to these hospitals.

At St. Mary's, the three floors added atop the west section of the hospital included one of the largest and best-equipped obstetrics departments in the area. There must have been something special in those days about three-story additions atop west wings – after the St. Mary's job was completed, Providence Hospital in Kansas City, Kan., hired J.E. Dunn in 1957 to do the same to its medical center. The market for new hospitals was a good one for J.E. Dunn, as well.

School construction and church work, mainstays for J.E. Dunn in earlier years, kept the construction company even busier during the 1950s. The baby boomers were being born in record numbers in the United States after the war and schools could hardly be built fast enough to make room for them all. In addition to new schools, families moving out to newly formed suburbs wanted places of worship built in their neighborhoods. J.E. Dunn cranked out classrooms and churches to meet the demand. It added a new church hall and more classrooms at St. Elizabeth's parish in Kansas City in 1949, constructed Our Lady of Lourdes elementary school and convent in Raytown in 1952, and made extensive additions to Christ the King parochial school in Kansas City in 1955. The company finished both the $1.8 million Van Horn High School and St. Mary's Elementary School in Independence in 1953. It completed construction on Bishop Miege High School in Roeland Park, Kan., in August 1958, a few weeks before breaking ground on a new elementary school for Visitation parish in Kansas City. By the start of the 1959 school year, J.E. Dunn had also built George Caleb Bingham Junior High School near the Waldo neighborhood in Kansas City.

The First Negotiated Contracts

*I*n the mid-1950s, J.E. Dunn built several parochial schools and Catholic churches north of the Missouri River. The work began when the construction company bid low for building an addition to St. Therese Little Flower Parish School in Parkville. The quality of J.E. Dunn's work on the Parkville school impressed the new bishop, John P. Cody, who then wanted J.E. Dunn to build all the diocesan projects. Bill suggested that the decision on which contractor to use should be left to the individual parishes. At the bishop's urging, however, several parishes negotiated work with J.E. Dunn. Under the terms of their agreement, J.E. Dunn would charge actual cost on the job plus a fixed fee; all savings would be returned to each individual parish.

The negotiated work that followed marked a major departure for J.E. Dunn. Until that time, the construction company had usually been one of many companies to bid on a given job. During this time,

however, owners – the parishes in this case – scrapped the bidding process and called on J.E. Dunn to do their work. The construction company performed more than a dozen negotiated jobs for the diocese including a new church for St. Charles parish in Gladstone; St. Michael's school and church and St. Pius X High School, both in North Kansas City; and St. James School in Liberty. It also remodeled the interior of the Cathedral of the Immaculate Conception in downtown Kansas City in 1955. When other construction companies were doing a diocesan project, Bishop Cody often tapped J.E. Dunn for free advice. "We would review architectural plans and specifications for the bishop, telling him how he could save money," says Bill. "This frustrated many architects who wondered where the bishop was getting his information."

The halls of higher education also had work for the construction company in the 1950s. J.E. Dunn added an auditorium and classrooms at Missouri State Teachers College in Kirksville, built the student union building and men's dormitory at William Jewell College, and finished dormitories and a cafeteria at the University of Missouri at Columbia, all during 1957 and 1958. The William Jewell projects marked the first time J.E. Dunn worked for a religious institution that wasn't Catholic. The construction company returned to William Jewell in 1964 to build a million dollar library. Also,

longtime client Rockhurst College hadn't forgotten J.E. Dunn, selecting the company in 1953 to build a $600,000 faculty residence hall for its Jesuit teachers and two dormitories later in the decade.

A Critical Hire

*T*hough he didn't know it at the time, Ernie Sr. made one of the best hiring decisions in the company's history when he hired a 19-year-old college student to be a timekeeper on the Rockhurst job. The athletic director at the college, Father Paul Smith, had asked Ernie to find a job for his nephew, Bernard Jacquinot, who had grown up on a farm in southeast Kansas. Bernard, a sophomore, reported for work that fall to Charlie Wakeman, superintendent of the Rockhurst project. Bernard found it wasn't easy to accommodate both his school schedule and his construction job, especially during his junior and senior years. "On Fridays, when I was supposed to turn in my time sheets, I had to attend mandatory Mass at the college at 8 a.m. and then attend classes until 3 p.m. One of the company's other two timekeepers, Virgil Black or Jess Hunt, would pick up the records from my desk and take them to the office."

Bernard Jacquinot has worked at J.E. Dunn more years than anyone except for Bill Dunn Sr.

The year 1956 sticks out in Bernard's mind. He was the timekeeper for the company's construction of Archbishop Edward J. Hunkeler's residence at 34th Street and Minnesota Avenue in Kansas City, Kan. "J.E. Dunn Sr. had done the estimating on that project and got so exasperated when the costs ran over the budget that he swore it was the last job he would ever estimate."

Coincidentally, and perhaps fortuitously, Bernard graduated from Rockhurst the same year with a degree in accounting. After working in the field for J.E. Dunn one more year and serving a two-year stint in the Army – during which time the construction company hired Cy Young to do its accounting and Beverly Kidder as a bookkeeper – Bernard returned from the service and asked for an office position. Ernie Sr. gave him a job working as an assistant to Gene Payne doing accounts payable work. In his new position, Bernard excelled in putting construction bids together.

"Bernard turned out to probably be the best estimator we've ever had," says Bill Dunn. Today, Bernard helps direct both the field operations and the warehouse. He provides the company's closest link between its office and field operations. Other than Bill Dunn Sr., no one has put in more years for the company.

Jim Crow Laws, Red Threats, and the Housing Authority

During the 1950s, Bernard and other J.E. Dunn employees were devoting much of their attention to public housing jobs. As the decade opened, Kansas City lagged behind other Midwestern cities in its public housing efforts. After completing low-income housing projects in St. Louis and Denver about ten years before, J.E. Dunn began building the Kansas City area's first public housing development, the Riverview Apartments in northeast Kansas City, after turning in a low bid of $1,709,242 on the project in the fall of 1951. Without making any apologies for institutionalized segregation, the Housing Authority of Kansas City designated all 232 dwelling units at Riverview for white families only. This seemed fair to members of the Housing Authority who had plans to build another public housing project in Kansas City for "Negro families." The Denver and St. Louis

housing authorities adhered to the same segregationist policy.

There wasn't any shortage of tenants at the Riverview Apartments. The Housing Authority decided to build another "whites only" apartment complex nearly twice as large to house all the eligible tenants on the Riverview waiting list. In January 1954, a year after completing the Riverview Apartments, J.E. Dunn was named general contractor on the $5 million, 454-unit Guinotte Manor project. The experience that J.E. Dunn had gained building the pre-war and World War II public housing projects probably helped the construction company win the bidding on many of Kansas City's public housing jobs done after the war, such as Guinotte Manor and later Chouteau Court.

As Dunn carried on with its public housing work, the nation's political climate veered to the right. U.S. Senator Joseph McCarthy was in his heyday, alerting Americans to the presence of Communists in their midst. Heeding his message, the Housing Authority required applicants for Guinotte Manor housing "to sign affidavits they are not Communists or members of any subversive organization."[7]

The Pittsburgh Plate Glass warehouse was a project involving tilt-up walls.

Challenges and Innovations in Commercial and Industrial Work

While public housing and other traditional markets stayed strong for J.E. Dunn in the 1950s, the company also branched into commercial and industrial markets. None of these "new market" jobs were particularly large, but a few had interesting challenges, and others were somewhat dangerous, with sad consequences. The Pittsburgh Plate Glass warehouse at Burlington Street and 12th Avenue in North Kansas City provided one of those challenges, giving the construction company its first experience with tilt-up walls. The proposed building was a one-story, reinforced concrete structure that covered 52,000 square feet. The architect/engineers on the project, Everett-Bleistein Associates, decided that the building's exterior, made up of 38 concrete wall panels weighing about seven tons apiece, would be poured and cured on the concrete floor before being "tilted" into position with motorized cranes.

Unfortunately, the Pittsburgh Plate Glass warehouse project was also a dangerous job, costing the life of J.R. "Rhode" Fisher, a carpenter foreman

for J.E. Dunn. Fisher was signaling to a hoisting engineer in one of the cranes to lower its boom. The hoisting engineer hit the wrong lever, causing the boom to touch some overhead power lines, and Fisher was electrocuted. It would not be the last J.E. Dunn job where a crane foul-up had deadly consequences.

Water became the challenge for J.E. Dunn crews in 1951. Nonstop rains that July caused the Kaw River to overflow its banks and flood both the industrial sections of Kansas City, Kan., and the West Bottoms in Kansas City, Mo. Bill Dunn arrived by rowboat to inspect the damage at the Hinde & Dauch box plant where the construction company had worked a few years earlier. He saw where floodwaters had risen as high as the second floor of the building. The cleanup effort at the box factory and at other J.E. Dunn jobs in Kansas City, Kan., became the construction company's first priority.

On jobs where Mother Nature was more accommodating, sometimes the challenge came from building designers who were abandoning traditional styles of architecture for more modern, geometric designs. One of those J.E. Dunn projects, the Dewey Portland Cement Co. building, located north of 47th Street on Belleview Avenue and now the offices of the Accurso Law Firm, might be mistaken

An aerial view of Guinotte Manor housing project.

When Ernie Sr. helped Bill manage the Guinotte Manor project, the biggest challenge they faced was the Housing Authority's board. Various members of the board had irked the Dunns on earlier public housing jobs, but they crossed the line with Ernie Sr. at Guinotte Manor when they tried to get the construction company to pick up the cost for their own mistakes.

At a meeting held in the field office, the head of the board announced to Ernie Sr. and Bill that the construction plans showed that 3/8 inch of plaster being applied to sheet rock throughout the units were superseded by the specs, which showed a 1/2 inch plaster application instead. "You owe us an 1/8 inch of plaster," the head of the board told them.

Ernie Sr. knew that an extra 1/8 inch of plaster would cost the construction company an astronomical amount of money. "I know one thing," Ernie Sr. shouted back across the table, "I know you're a bunch of goddam SOB's." Then he stormed out.

Later Bill settled matters peaceably with the Housing Authority at his father's request, and the construction company made a profit on the job. Despite the flap, J.E. Dunn and the Housing Authority worked together again during construction of the Chouteau Court and the Pennway Plaza, both begun in 1958, and Wayne Miner, started in 1959.

*Poolside at Mission Hills
Country Club.*

for a Frank Lloyd Wright design. The actual architects, Edward W. Tanner & Associates, designed it to emphasize the owner's line of business. Built in 1955, the building featured reinforced concrete with architectural concrete walls. On its upper floors, cantilevered canopies – also made of architectural concrete – extended over a continuous bank of windows. J.E. Dunn normally didn't have to worry about the appearance of its concrete work; concrete was for support, not aesthetics. Here, the challenge was to minimize any visible flaws in the final architectural concrete

walls to give them the appearance of cut stone. With railing work framing a deck on its top floor and a series of horizontal windows stacked one story upon another, the building looked like a small ocean liner moored on a spit of grass. The Dewey Portland Cement Building marked the third commercial building that J.E. Dunn had built on the west side of the Plaza during the 1950s. The two other structures, the A.B. Sinclair Building, just south of the Dewey building, and the Skelly Oil addition on 47th Street, had already opened their doors for business.

The more J.E. Dunn ventured into the commercial and industrial markets, the more its reputation grew for doing quality work. Its superintendents continued to impress owners and architects with their thoroughness. Gerry Stroud was one such superintendent. In 1955, Stroud was the general superintendent for a 55,000 square foot addition to the Townley Metal and Hardware Co. building at Third and Walnut streets. Bill Dunn remembers that when he asked the architect's representative for a punch list on the $500,000 building, he was told, "There is no punch list. Your superintendent was much more demanding and tougher than the architect would have been."

Many J.E. Dunn superintendents and their crews found themselves working in a variety of settings during the 1950s. Their assignments sometimes took them to posh, suburban neighborhoods, particularly after another market opened up for the construction company: country clubs. The work began when J.E. Dunn installed a swimming pool for Homestead Country Club in 1953. After submitting the low bid to Mission Hills Country Club in 1955, J.E. Dunn built a new contemporary-styled clubhouse, designed by the Kivett & Myers architectural firm. J.E. Dunn and the same architects teamed up again in 1957 for the $1 million general offices of the Missouri Public Service Co. on U.S. 50 Highway, southeast of Raytown. By then, the firm had renamed itself Kivett & Myers & McCallum. Kivett et. al. won awards for their design of the Missouri Public Service headquarters, a glass boxlike building that featured exterior louvers and five-foot concrete overhangs to help control "greenhouse effect" heating from the sun and glare. By the early 1960s, the contemporary look promoted by Kivett and other architects, had gained widespread acceptance.

When Blue Hills Country Club decided to move from an older neighborhood to a new site at 127th Street and State Line Road, it went for the same sleek look, choosing the design of Linscott, Kiene and Haylett. Both the Mission Hills and Blue Hills architects opted to paint their clubhouse exteriors in blinding shades of white; even the native stone walls at Blue Hills were "whited out." A veteran in country club construction by then, J.E. Dunn finished the $2.25 million Blue Hills project in December 1963.

The Missouri Public Service Building won design awards for the architectural firm of Kivett & Myers & McCallum.

J.E. Dunn Goes On Tour

*B*y the mid-1950s, Ernie Sr.'s career path had taken many unusual turns. He had been a semi-professional baseball player, electrical supply salesman, building contractor, and real estate builder. Now in his early sixties, Ernie Sr. added one more title to his varied resume: chairman of Kansas City's first goodwill tour of Latin America. In its Nov. 11, 1955 edition, *The Kansas City Star* announced that Ernie was among 30 local business leaders appointed to serve a three-year term on Mayor H. Roe Bartle's Commission for International Relations.

Commission members made it clear that their Latin American mission didn't stop when they returned to Kansas City. A *New York Herald Tribune* reporter quoted Ernie: "We didn't go down there to plant

a seed and let it die. We have just begun. We're going to keep working at this through our city, and Washington as well." Less than a month after their return home, Mayor Bartle, Hal Hendrix, Ernie, and two other members of the commission flew to Washington, D.C., where they met with State, Treasury, and Commerce Department officials and testified before a Senate committee about their fact-finding tour. The Kansas Citians presented government officials with a list of what they thought Latin American countries needed most from the United States, including loans for schools and roads, easier credit terms with our country, and having more U.S. business and technical know-how offered to their countries. Asked why the United States should be helping Latin American countries, Ernie replied, "Because we need them more than they need us."

THE KANSAS CITY STAR. T

MISSOURI CONGRESSIONAL DELEGATION MEMBERS PLAYED HOSTS today in Washington to leaders of Kansas City's business and civic delegation who are on their way to South America for a tour of that continent. This picture, made at a breakfast meeting, shows (seated, from left) Senator Stuart Symington, Mayor H. Roe Bartle and J. E. Dunn, chairman of the Kansas City commission for international relations and trade, and (standing, left) Representative William R. Hull, Jr., Weston, Mo., and Representative Richard Bolling of Kansas City—(Wirephoto).

Before leaving for South America in February 1956, Kansas City Mayor H. Roe Bartle (center) and Ernie Dunn Sr., chairman of the Latin American Tour and Commission (seated to his right), met with Missouri U.S. Senator Stuart Symington (seated left) and Missouri U.S. Representatives William R. Hull Jr. of Weston (standing left) and Richard Bolling of Kansas City (standing right).

The idea for a Latin American Commission and Tour came from Hal Hendrix, a young journalist who wrote a Latin American column for the *Kansas City Star*. He recommended that Mayor Bartle select Ernie Dunn as its chairman. Hendrix, who would win a Pulitzer Prize in 1963 for his articles on the Cuban Missile Crisis and Latin American coverage while working for the *Miami News*, explained why he suggested Ernie Dunn for chairman: "I knew he wouldn't be self-aggrandizing, tooting his own horn."

As chairman of the delegation, Ernie was expected to introduce the mayor to businessmen, heads of state, and other dignitaries at social functions in the various countries. "Ernie was usually quite serious when he spoke on those occasions," recalls Hendrix who went along on the tour as *The Star's* reporter. "Bartle would add levity when he spoke after Ernie's introduction. He'd often make fun of his own size." Bartle weighed more than 300 pounds. When the tour came to Uruguay, some of the local Communist newspapers called him "the Great White Whale."

Bartle and his troops seemed to leave a favorable impression in every country they visited. Along the way, they handed out more than 100 gold keys to Kansas City and cartons of heart-shaped stickers that read "Heart of America" with "Kansas City" printed below. Political leaders, such as Brazilian Vice President Joao Goulart,

accepted invitations from commission members to visit Kansas City. The commission hosted 17 Latin American ambassadors at the American Royal Ball and other events in Kansas City that next October.

A Latin American tour from Kansas City might not sound important today, but things were different in 1956 with the Cold War running in high gear. Political commentators, who saw the Soviet Union vying for influence in Central and South America, praised the Kansas City delegation. "Kansas City seems to have the answer to Moscow's recently announced economic penetration of Latin America," wrote Daniel James for the *New York Herald Tribune*. "Its answer is not to wait for federal action, but to act on your own. As a result, it has jumped with both feet into the tense international arena, and become the first American municipality to send a friendship-and-trade delegation to Latin America."

Kansas City Tim

KANSAS CITY, MAY 14, 1957—TUESDAY—34 PAGES.

RICARDO MANUEL ARIAS, AMBASSADOR OF PANAMA, and Mrs. Arias arrived here yesterday from Washington and were greeted at the Municipal Air Terminal by civic leaders. Shown are (left to right) J. E. Dunn, former president of the Kansas City Association for International Relations and Trade; Francis J. FitzPatrick, former president of the Chamber of Commerce; Mrs. Arias, receiving a bouquet of roses; Arias, former ambassador of the republic; and the Very Rev. Maurice E. Van Ackeren, president of Rockhurst college. (Story on page 3.)

Ernie Dunn Sr. (left) welcomes Panamanian Ambassador Ricardo Manuel Arias (second from right) and his wife to Kansas City. Joining them at Municipal Airport are former president of the Kansas City Chamber of Commerce Francis J. FitzPatrick (second from left) and Father Maurice E. Van Ackeren, president of Rockhurst College (far right).

In January 1957, patent lawyer C. Earl Hovey succeeded Ernie as chairman of the commission; Ernie became its first president. Later that year, when the commission took a trip to Central America, Ernie was on the tour, pitching again for his hometown. Ernie used his connections with the Latin American commission to get the Panamanian ambassador, Ricardo Manuel Arias, to come to Kansas City in May 1957. The ambassador spoke at Rockhurst College, where Ernie had recently been named chairman of the board of regents. Through Ernie's efforts, both the city and the college gained from the ambassador's trip.

Likewise, Ernie accomplished two goals when he was named the building trade's co-chairman of the Heart of America United Campaign in 1958: raising money for charities and promoting the image of the local construction industry by showing how its contractors and trades people were concerned with the overall welfare of the community. The United Campaign, now known as the United Way Campaign, is a cause J.E. Dunn Construction has backed ever since its founder first got involved.

In addition to his involvement with the United Campaign and the Commission for International Relations, Ernie devoted time and talent to the Don Bosco Community Center, a youth center on Kansas City's northeast side. Two buddies from his baseball days, Alex Nigro and Vince Dasta, got Ernie interested in the cause, which was close to their hearts. Ernie joined the Don Bosco board of directors in the late 1950s. Since then, the community center has expanded its services to include helping immigrants settle in the area and meeting the needs of the elderly. The construction company continues to support the center to this day.

The 1960s: An Era Comes to a Close

Happy Days, the title of a popular television about teenagers growing up in the early 1960s, sums up how many people feel about the era. The country was at peace, though a little shaken with Cold War jitters. After two decades of being strapped for cash, white-collar Americans were finally enjoying a little prosperity in spacious suburbia. Critics of the era point out that the working classes continued to struggle – construction laborers made about two dollars an hour in the early 1960s – and that white suburbanites tended to forget the plight of poor minority groups they had left behind in the cities. Labor unions and civil rights leaders tried to stake out a better life for their constituents and sometimes succeeded – the U.S. Supreme Court ruled in 1954 that schools could no longer be segregated – but significant results wouldn't come until an altogether different era. For the moment, most Americans were preoccupied with making money and giving their children a taste of "the good life."

At J.E. Dunn, many of the World War II veterans had learned the ropes by now and were rising to positions of leadership in the office and the field. Jack McCollom, Bill Miller, Charlie Wakeman, Woody Randolph, John Spencer, Dick Neumann and Gerry Stroud had all become superintendents by the mid-1960s. In the office, Ernie Sr. kept up on new construction work as it came along, but he was often happy to let his sons run the show. For their part, the two sons tried to balance their work with their family obligations. By the mid-1960s, Ernie Jr. had seven sons and one daughter and Bill had five sons. Always an enthusiastic outdoorsman, Ernie Jr. would take his sons hunting and fishing.

By contrast, Bill was never a nature lover like his brother – all those weekends spent working on his parents' farm in Stanley had ruined it for him. Bill was a good sport though, taking his boys on annual fishing trips to Table Rock Lake in Missouri or to Minnesota, but he preferred competitive sports. He coached the baseball and football teams for which his three oldest boys, Bill Jr., Terry, and Steve, played. In contrast to Rose Dunn's household, where academic achievement always rated highest, competitive sports won hands down in Bill and Jean's house. Four of Bill's sons followed in his and their grandfather's footsteps, coaching sports teams at the end of the workday. Steve, who used to dream of being a high school history teacher and varsity football coach, was honored at St. Agnes parish for being a grade school football coach for 25 years.

Sometimes, when Ernie Sr. watched his grandchildren play sports, he did his own brand of coaching. During the last inning of a Cub Scout baseball game, for example, his grandson, Terry, had just driven in the winning run for his team. "I won the game! I won the game!" he shouted to his Grandpa Dunn. His grandfather was quick to correct him, "It was the whole team's effort that won the game." Today, when Terry and his brothers describe the J.E. Dunn philosophy for doing business, they use phrases that underscore "the team effort" and the importance of "giving it

An inside look at a tremie used to keep spring water from rushing in to displace concrete poured for a drilled pier at Wayne Miner Court.

your all." Clearly they are repeating lessons learned at an early age.

Ernie Sr. stayed active almost to the time of his passing in 1964. After his term as president of Kansas City's Latin American Commission ended, Ernie remained a goodwill ambassador, hosting international students who were being schooled locally and even standing in as "father of the bride" to give a Brazilian woman of Chinese descent in marriage to her Taiwanese groom. The bride, Mrs. Juin Sheng Yu, told reporters, "Mr. Dunn has always been a friend of foreign students."[8] In his free time, Ernie Sr. loved to shop for antiques with Rose. "He liked the antiques more than she did," says his daughter, Mary Ellen. "He used to say, 'I don't drink, smoke, or chase wild women. Going to antique auctions is my only vice.'"

Wayne Miner

Even though he spent more time at work on real estate matters during his last years, Ernie Sr. would still get excited about the construction side of his business, especially when projects as big as Wayne Miner came along. Kansas City hadn't seen anything in public housing that was close to the size of Wayne Miner Court. Plans called for a total of 738 apartment units in three 10-story and two nine-story apartment houses, plus 15 two-story garden-type buildings. J.E. Dunn beat out eight other contractors for the Wayne Miner project, submitting a bid of $8,900,258 to the Housing Authority of Kansas City on January 31, 1959. The five brick and concrete high rises were the first of their kind in urban renewal programming west of Chicago. Both white and black families would be eligible to move into the low-

The Wayne Miner public housing project consisted of three 10-story apartment buildings, two nine-story apartment buildings, and 15 garden-type apartment buildings.

Coach Bill Dunn Jr. holds a trophy won by the Cure' of Ars seventh and eighth grade girls' track team in 1991. (L-R): Elizabeth Wristen, Bill, Jamie Calcara, Maureen Hurley, and Amy Dunn (Bill's daughter).

If there is an analogy to the J.E. Dunn approach to leadership, it is to be found in coaching. While many companies and executives, the Dunns included, utilize sports and teamwork analogies, Bill Sr. and four of his sons draw actively and regularly on their coaching background.

The tradition goes as far back as the company itself. Speaking of his father, Ernie Dunn Sr., Bill Dunn Sr. remembers: "All the kids in the block used to wait for him to come home at night…there were a lot of times we would play softball in our backyard and he would pitch and play with us. And then he coached the grade school baseball teams that my brother played on…he loved all kinds of sports. He was a fierce competitor."

Of his own playing career, Bill Sr. says, "I'm grateful I played football in college. That's where I learned that when you get knocked down you pick yourself back up again and keep on playing."

In kind, Steve Dunn remembers his father's, Bill Sr.'s, coaching days and style. The comparisons to the senior Dunn's approach to business are impossible to miss. "The first time he coached me it was for a baseball team. He didn't show favoritism as a coach. 'You're going to have to play twice as well as the guy ahead of you if you want to play,' he told me. He was patient. He was a stickler for fundamentals – doing it the right way."

Steve also remembers that it wasn't always easy being the coach's son. "I was holding my wrist after making a tackle as a defensive end for St. Agnes Grade School. When I told my dad on the sidelines how much it hurt, he told me that it looked OK to him and kept me in for the rest of the game." The doctor had a different diagnosis the next day: the wrist was broken. Steve followed their grandfather and father onto the sidelines, coaching for over 25 years at St. Agnes.

Bill Jr. was a youth league football coach for over twenty years and also coached track. His experience of his father as a coach concurs with Steve's. "[Dad] was one of my baseball coaches when I played for the St. Regis Raiders in about fifth grade.

He was tougher on me than the other kids on the team. He was always tougher on his own sons because he wanted to prepare us for life."

Terry also participated in the family avocation. "I spent several years volunteering as a football coach for grade school and high school teams. In my work, I find myself drawing on the skills I learned as a coach and those I learned from mentors such as my father, Bill Dunn Sr."

rent apartment complex at Eleventh Street and Euclid Avenue. The days of segregated public housing were over.

Bill remembers the surprise waiting for J.E. Dunn crews on the job when they tried to pour concrete for drilled piers: "Water would gush up from underground and wash out the newly poured concrete. We found out that a spring that fed into Turkey Creek ran right under the site." The construction company solved the problem by pouring the concrete through tremies, large round hoses inserted through steel shafts.

Work progressed and the first tenants began moving in by the next winter. At a dedication for the apartment complex, U.S. Rep. Richard Bolling of Missouri praised the Wayne Miner buildings. "Such projects benefit everyone in this area because they provide healthful and economical living space," he said. Time would prove him wrong. Like so many other publicly funded high rises across the country, Wayne Miner would become a breeding ground for crime and unsanitary living conditions. Some conservatives like to blame the Kennedy and Johnson administrations for these costly blunders in public housing, but Republican Dwight Eisenhower was still in office when ground was broken at Wayne Miner. Forty years later, demolition experts would turn the

high-rise buildings to rubble in a matter of minutes.

When the construction of Wayne Miner Court was finished in 1961, it marked a turning point for J.E. Dunn. A staple of the construction company for the previous two decades, the government housing jobs all but dried up after its completion. The company's involvement in apartment construction in general would also taper off after Swope Crestview, a 60-unit apartment complex, was finished that summer. Though residential markets slowed down, other traditional markets such as school and hospital construction gained new vigor. Commercial work came in at a slow but steady pace with jobs such as an expansion and renovation at Kansas City's Downtown Municipal Airport.

Suburban Sprawl

*T*he continued rush to the suburbs in the 1960s fueled much of the construction company's work. In 1961, J.E. Dunn built the new St. John LaLande church and grade school in Blue Springs, Mo., a rural town east of Kansas City being overtaken by suburbia. In Lenexa, Kan., at the western edge of the metropolitan area, the construction company was building a new school for Holy Trinity parish, where Bill and Ernie Jr.'s

grandfather and great-uncle, Henry and Theodore Bruening, had erected a stone church more than 80 years before.

When longtime area Catholic schools, Rockhurst High and Notre Dame de Sion Academy, decided to move away from older neighborhoods in Kansas City, J.E. Dunn won the bidding for their work. The new Rockhurst High School building opened at 93rd Street and State Line Road in 1962, the same year Sion students began attending school at 106th Terrace and Wornall Road. About this same time, the Catholic Diocese of Kansas City-St. Joseph decided to build a school for children with learning disabilities. With J.E. Dunn as its general contractor, the Marillac School of Special Education was dedicated in January 1963 on land just north of the Sion school.

Other area parochial schools and churches avoided the rush to the suburbs, choosing instead to update and expand their existing facilities. J.E. Dunn added three stories onto St. Pius X High School in North Kansas City in 1962, built an addition for Blessed Sacrament Church, and renovated Holy Rosary School in northeast Kansas City and St. Michael the Archangel Church at 24th Street and Brighton Avenue during this period.

Rural Construction and Rural Commuters

The boom in diocesan construction wasn't limited to the city and the suburbs. Residents of small towns across Kansas and Missouri saw J.E. Dunn crews at work in the early 1960s, building new Catholic schools and churches in their communities. They built the Holy Rosary parish center in Clinton, Mo.; St. Patrick's Church in Butler, Mo.; and a new school for Holy Family Parish in Eudora, Kan. Much larger jobs came from college and university towns outside the Kansas City area. J.E. Dunn built an electrical engineering building for the University of Missouri in Columbia in 1960 and completed a men's dormitory at Central Missouri State College in Warrensburg in 1961. Central Missouri State went through a growth spurt in the 1960s and J.E. Dunn crews, led by Bill Miller as their superintendent, performed much of its construction work throughout the decade.

In the more rural areas of Kansas, the construction company built a dormitory at St. Mary's, a Catholic women's college near Leavenworth, and completed work on the $2 million St. John's Hospital in Leavenworth in March 1963.

While rural communities were providing more construction work for J.E. Dunn in the late 1950s and early 1960s, they were also becoming prime sources for some of J.E. Dunn's best construction workers. Thus began the era of the long commute for many company employees. Several members of the Corlew family and Charlie and Curtis Wakeman drove to work from their homes near Oak Grove, Mo. Bill Miller traveled from Pleasant Hill, Mo. Jim Griffin and some of his relatives commuted from Orrick, Mo. Dick Neumann made a daily trek from Atchison. Labor foreman Everett Reynolds traveled from Warrensburg, Mo., and Bill Dunn remembers that many workers that traveled from as far away as Sedalia, Mo. They were an energetic bunch. Besides putting in 40 or more hours a week on construction sites, many of these men spent evenings and weekends working on their family farms. And their on-the-job work was just about as hard and backbreaking as it had been for construction workers before World War II. Some of the more significant labor saving devices and methods wouldn't show up on construction sites for at least another decade. The materials used in building, however, were already changing.

J.E. Dunn bid for work at Mount St. Scholastica, a Catholic women's college in Atchison, Kan., where the company had worked before World War II, but the Mount St. Scholastica work was not meant to be this time around. During the trip to Atchison to submit the bid, while Ernie Sr. sped along in a big Buick and Bill Dunn and Gene Payne reviewed numbers in the backseat, the car struck a sow and her piglets at a crest of the road. A few of the little pigs died instantly. "I won't come back this way," Ernie said, "because a farmer will be waiting here with a shotgun."

They arrived in Atchison and placed the bid just as the deadline bells began to ring, but ended up being outbid anyway. On the bright side, there were no incidents of gunfire on an alternate route back to Kansas City.

J.E. Dunn updated Kansas City's Downtown Airport in the early 1960s.

Milestones

*T*he *Kansas City Star* noted one of the building materials changes in a June 4, 1961 article covering J.E. Dunn's construction of yet another big parking garage for downtown developer Joe Bruening. The garage incorporated what the reporter called "unusual" precast, prestressed, and post-tensioned concrete beams. The compressed concrete used on the job made the supporting beams much stronger and more resilient than ordinary concrete. The construction company completed the three-level parking facility at the southwest corner of 10th and Wyandotte by the end of that summer. A few months later, J.E. Dunn was at work on another building associated with Joe Bruening, converting his former mansion in Liberty into a retreat house for the Kansas City-St. Joseph Diocese. The Immacolata Retreat House hadn't been opened long when Joe Bruening, Rose Dunn's youngest brother, died on June 25, 1963. By the end of the decade, an entire generation of Dunns and Bruenings would be gone except for Rose, who died in 1974.

While one generation passed away, the construction company continued to build hospitals for the larger World War II and baby boom generations taking its place. J.E. Dunn completed a $3.5 million expansion and renovation at the old St. Joseph Hospital at Linwood Boulevard and Prospect Avenue. The Sisters of St. Joseph of Carondelet, who operated the hospital, were celebrating its 90th anniversary in 1964 while construction crews refurbished its power plant, laboratories, lounge, and dining facilities. Just west of Saint Luke's Hospital near the Plaza, J.E. Dunn completed the $3 million Medical Plaza office building in January 1963 and began work on Saint Luke's itself. Saint Luke's plans for a $7 million expansion and modernization were extensive. The hospital contracted with J.E. Dunn to add a new eight-story wing that would include 185 beds and surgical, X-ray, therapeutic, and diagnostic units. The front of Saint Luke's flip-flopped with its back so that the entrance would be on Wornall Road facing the new medical office building instead of J.C. Nichols Parkway. The last phase of construction would add a new entrance building with a lobby, admitting office, chapel, and coffee and gift shops to the Wornall Road side.

Doing the Lord's Work

*T*he St. Joseph and Saint Luke's jobs were profitable ones for J.E. Dunn, but sometimes Ernie Sr. had a more charitable purpose in mind when building

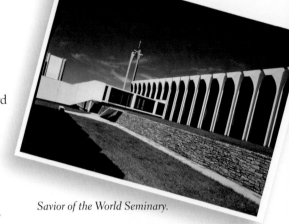

Savior of the World Seminary.

facilities that cared for the sick and elderly. For example, the construction company didn't charge a fee for any of the projects done in the 1950s and early 1960s for the Spanish nuns who ran Our Lady of Mercy retirement home at Ninth and Harrison streets.

Organized religion became one of the pillars of the establishment under attack in this country during the late 1960s, but in the more conservative days of the early 1960s, most Americans still looked to their churches for guidance. Attendance in parochial schools was at an all-time high and record numbers of young adults were eager to become ministers, priests, and nuns. J.E. Dunn's workload reflected this national trend. Besides building one parochial school after another, the construction company picked up several jobs building housing facilities for clergymen and people studying for the ministry. J.E. Dunn built a new rectory to house priests at Christ the King parish in Kansas City in 1961 and began construction on a convent for St. Joseph parish in

Shawnee, Kan., the next year. Other denominations in the Kansas City area had housing needs, too. In June 1963, J.E. Dunn completed a $403,000 men's dormitory at the Midwest Baptist Theological Seminary on North Oak Trafficway.

Less than a year later, the construction company submitted a low bid to build Savior of the World Catholic Seminary on farmland in western Wyandotte County, Kan. The seminary would be the first diocesan preparatory school for future priests in Kansas. The six-building complex, designed in a combination of traditional and modern styles, was an award winner for its architects, Shaughnessy, Bower & Grimaldi. Each of its two-story buildings was lined with precast arches made of white cement, sand, and quartz aggregate etched to expose the quartz elements. Ernie Sr.'s friend, John P. Cody, who had become archbishop of Chicago, would preside at the seminary's dedication in October 1966, but Ernie himself didn't live long enough to see the project completed.

The End of an Era

Ernie's death on Dec. 31, 1964 didn't come as complete surprise. He'd had a heart attack two years earlier, after which he'd gone on a diet, but the damage to his coronary system was already too great. The second attack came in mid-December, and he seemed to be recuperating at St. Mary's Hospital on the morning he died. At the funeral held at Our Lady of Good Counsel Church two days later, all his pallbearers were employees of the construction company: Cy Young, Charlie Banister, Jack McCollom, Charlie Wakeman, Woody Randolph, Bill Miller, Gene Payne, and Bernard Jacquinot. Outside his own family, they were the people to whom he was closest. Rose, the wife who was always so different from him in temperament, felt his loss most keenly. Good friends like Father Maurice Van Ackeren, president of Rockhurst College, and Father Joseph Freeman, another Jesuit priest from the college, helped her through two difficult years following his death. After the long grieving period, Rose emerged as a more extroverted and fun-loving person than she had ever been before. Her husband, who'd always been proud of her, would have marveled at the transformation.

At the time of his death, Ernie's construction company had a net worth of $1.4 million. As part of his estate planning, he devised that shares in the company be divided equally among his four children and his wife. The will made no mention of his greatest legacies: the example he'd shown in his own life and his philosophy of doing business. "My father had seen people struggling all of his life and felt motivated to help them," Bill says. "He could have made a lot of money during World War II but opted to turn any profits on defense work back to the government and often did construction work for religious organizations at cost. He was a lot like my father-in-law, Charlie Aylward, who never took a large salary when he became chairman of the Columbia National Bank and was later co-chairman of Columbia Union Bank. Both of them could have been very rich men but that wasn't terribly important to them."

Some of the things that mattered most to Ernie were treating clients and employees fairly and with respect. "Anyone can build a building. There's a lot of people doing it," Ernie once told Bill. "It's how you do the job and whether the design team and owner want you back again that is going to determine whether you stay in business." About the people who work for you Ernie had this to say: "Get the best people you can get, give them interesting and challenging work, and let them share whatever rewards there are in the company." Those little bits of fatherly advice still guide the construction company nearly 40 years after its founder's death.

Rose and Ernie Dunn with their daughter-in-law, Jean Dunn, in early 1964. Ernie died less than a year later at age 71.

Chapter 3
LABOR PAINS
1964-1974

The Vista Del Rio retirement apartments at Cherry Street and Admiral Boulevard in Kansas City were important for two reasons: it was the first J.E. Dunn job to use a climbing crane and the project established peer review as a standard procedure for the construction company.

THE TURBULENT 1960s

Brothers in Arms

BY THE MID-1960S, THE "HAPPY DAYS" ERA IN AMERICA WAS OVER, REPLACED BY A TIME OF STRIFE AND PROTEST. THOUGH THE IMAGE OF A LONGHAIRED, FLAG-BURNING VIETNAM WAR PROTESTER MAY COME TO MIND, PROTESTERS ACTUALLY HAD MANY FACES AND MANY CAUSES. DR. MARTIN LUTHER KING JR. LED BLACK AMERICANS IN THEIR STRUGGLE FOR EQUALITY UNDER THE LAW UNTIL AN ASSASSIN'S BULLETS STOPPED HIM, LEAVING OTHER CIVIL RIGHTS LEADERS TO CONTINUE THE CAUSE. WOMEN, TIRED OF BEING TREATED LIKE SECOND-CLASS CITIZENS,

ORGANIZED THEMSELVES INTO THE WOMEN'S LIBERATION MOVEMENT. THE WINDS OF DISCONTENT SWEPT THROUGH THE NATION'S WORK FORCE, TOO. LABOR STRIKES BECAME EVERYDAY EVENTS, BUT THIS

TIME AROUND, THE UNIONS FORCED MANAGEMENT TO LISTEN. WORKING CONDITIONS IMPROVED AND WAGES ROSE, BUT SO DID INFLATION, WHICH BROUGHT A NEW ROUND OF PROBLEMS.

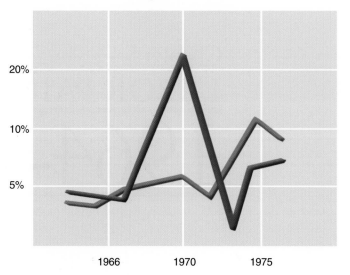

Wages vs. Inflation

— Carpenter wage % increase
— U.S. inflation

During the late 1960s and early 1970s, union construction workers in the Kansas City area saw the percentage increase in their wages spike far ahead of the national inflation rate. The graph shows inflation increasing at about 5.5 % in 1969 and about 6 % in 1970 while the hourly wage for union journeymen carpenters in Kansas City rose about 19 % and 23 % in those respective years. Source: The Kansas City Builders' Association.

L-R: Bernard Jacquinot, Ernie Dunn Jr., Bill Dunn Sr., Gene Payne, and Cy Young delve into construction blueprints.

*B*ill Dunn knew that something had to change at J.E. Dunn Construction before the 1960s had even dawned. All through the 1950s, the construction company competed in a hard-bid market where jobs went to the lowest bidder, whether or not that bidder was the best-qualified contractor for the project. It frustrated him to see J.E. Dunn as just one bidder among many. The hit-or-miss nature of the bidding market made it hard to predict what the company's volume of work would be from one year to the next. There'd been a few lean years for the company in the 1950s and that trend would continue into the 1960s. Eventually, J.E. Dunn would escape the hard bid treadmill, but only after the labor movement succeeded in turning the local construction industry on its ear in the late 1960s and early 1970s.

After Ernie Sr. died in December 1964, the immediate issue was what his spouse and four children would do with the construction company he'd left to them. By 1966, his two sons, Ernie Jr. and Bill, bought the shares in the business that were owned by their mother and two sisters. After selling her shares in J.E. Dunn, Mary Ellen, the older sister, moved to southern California with her husband, Roy Daly, and their eight children. There, they began a real estate development and management

company. They built and owned apartments in the Los Angeles suburbs just as that market was starting to boom. Of all Ernie Sr.'s children, Mary Ellen proved to be the smartest real estate developer. She knew better than her father the importance of location in the real estate market and excelled with her husband in property management. All the while they were living in California, the Dalys kept a house in the Kansas City area, where Mary Ellen now lives. Roy, her husband of 55 years, died in 2000.

After her buyout, the younger sister, Rosalie, moved to Fort Lauderdale, Fla., with her husband, Mike Donahue, and their three children. Once her children were a little older, Rosalie used the degree she earned in medical technology to work in a doctor's office in Florida. Like her older sister, Rosalie and her family returned later to live in Kansas City where Mike headed up real estate development for Farm and Home Savings & Loan and helped develop the Lakewood properties

near Lee's Summit. Rosalie and Mike were married 46 years when he died in 1997. There must be a construction gene that runs in the family: both Mary Ellen and Rosalie have sons who manage their own construction companies. Paul Daly builds houses in the Kansas City area, and Mickey Donahue is a homebuilder in Atlanta.

Once they bought out their mother and sisters, Ernie Jr. and Bill had to decide how they would run both the real estate and construction sides of the business. Ultimately, Ernie Jr. divided his time between real estate management and construction while Bill was involved almost entirely in construction. It had become apparent to their employees that the two brothers had different styles of doing business.

"Back when Bill and Ernie did all the estimating, Bill turned in bids at the last minute while Ernie turned in bids ahead of time," says Bernard Jacquinot. "Ernie was more detailed and spent considerable time documenting things, while Bill usually cut to the chase on documentation. Bill grasped things quickly and wasted no time making his point."

Former superintendent John Spencer saw a difference in temperament between the brothers: "When he thought something should be done differently on a job, Bill was diplomatic, more like his mother. Ernie tended to be more like his father." Bernard Jacquinot observed the same thing: "Ernie was sometimes more direct. Ernie and Bill might end up with similar resolutions, but they approached issues in different ways."

Ardyth Wendte, who began secretarial work for the construction company in the fall of 1966, remembers working well with both brothers, but like all the other J.E. Dunn employees from that era, Ardyth would have to choose between them when the split finally came.

Their different philosophies of doing business eventually led to Bill's offering to buy out his brother's interest in the company less than 10 years after their father's death. Many of the changes Bill wanted for the company had to wait until Ernie Jr. agreed to that buyout in 1974. The years in between, 1965 to 1974, were a turbulent time for the country and a challenging era for the construction company as well.

Ardyth Wendte, who began working for J.E. Dunn as a secretary in 1966, eventually became an officer of the company and head of its personnel department.

Both Ernie Jr. and Bill increased their civic involvement during the period, often stepping into roles their father had performed. Ernie Jr. was made second vice president of the Associated General Contractors in 1967 and would later become its president, a post his father held during World War II. Like his father before him, Bill became a member of the board of regents of Rockhurst College. Bill served on the St. Mary's Hospital Board and Ernie was elected president of the lay advisory board of St. Joseph Hospital in 1967. Bill Dunn became chair of the Catholic laymen's conference of the Catholic Archdiocese of Kansas City in Kansas and was elected to the board of directors of Columbia National Bank.

Bill also joined the local board of the Cerebral Palsy Foundation after his friends, Clark and Peg Murray, lost their teenage daughter to the disease. The problems faced by special needs people and their families hit close to home after Bill's wife, Jean, gave birth on November 4, 1967, to their last child and only daughter, Mary. The attending physician knew the baby had Down syndrome, but he couldn't tell that she also had a potentially fatal heart defect. A few days later, Bill was flying with his daughter to Washington, D.C., where a well-known doctor was trying out a new drug to improve mental functioning in

Down syndrome children. The drug never lived up to the claims.

Soon, little Mary's heart problems surfaced, necessitating surgery when she was only four months old. About a month later, Mary nearly died at home one weekend night. Her mother heard her in the next room, gasping for breath. "Her lips were peeled back and her skin had turned a bluish color," Jean remembers. Bill probably helped save Mary's life that night by breathing air into her mouth. Their oldest son, Bill Jr., who was just getting home from a date, heard the commotion and brought over a doctor who lived in the neighborhood.

Mary recovered at the University of Kansas Medical Center, but her parents have always wondered if the minutes she went without air had a permanent effect on her mental abilities. Today, Mary is more severely mentally impaired than most people with Down syndrome, functioning at the level of a two-year-old. She lives in a home for disabled women. Every other weekend, her parents bring her to their home, where "her father dotes on Mary," Jean says. As part of their routine, Bill drives Mary by construction sites and they often make the rounds at the J.E. Dunn main office on Saturday mornings. "Having Mary in my life has rearranged my priorities," Bill says. "It's strengthened my commitment toward helping the less fortunate."

The Calm Before the Storm

By turning over many of the day-to-day operations of J.E. Dunn Construction to his sons throughout the 1950s and 1960s, Ernie Sr. had prepared them for an easier transition after his death. Projects that were started before he died, such as the Saint Luke's Hospital additions and Savior of the World Seminary, went on without a hitch. Traditional markets for J.E. Dunn, such as hospital and school construction, a few commercial projects, and retirement apartments, brought a steady stream of work in the mid-1960s.

An old client, St. Mary's Hospital, found more work for J.E. Dunn in 1965 when it planned to convert the former Bruce Dodson Insurance Building into a new hospital wing. The plans would have appalled members of any local historic preservation organization, but that movement was still in its infancy. When the remodeling was completed in 1966, not a trace of the old exterior was visible. The landmark building's classical portico and enameled terra cotta walls were faced with brick panels and window screens of anodized aluminum. Area power plants had more appeal than the new exterior, but the laboratories, morgue, and offices

inside were just what the St. Mary's nuns had ordered. Architectural aesthetics didn't seem to rank high on the list of priorities in the mid-1960s. J.E. Dunn also churned out a particularly grim-looking three-story building in 1966 to house the archdiocesan chancery office in Kansas City, Kan.

Meanwhile, the Jesuits at Rockhurst College continued keeping J.E. Dunn crews busy on their campus. J.E. Dunn had beaten out 10 other bidders in December 1965 to build McGee Hall dormitory, a reinforced-concrete frame structure that was six stories high. The project marked a milestone for Terry Dunn. "I was 16 years old the summer of 1966, working as a laborer for J.E. Dunn for the first time," he remembers. Charlie Wakeman, the same superintendent that started Bernard Jacquinot on his first J.E. Dunn assignment at Rockhurst more than a decade before, met Terry on his first day of work. "I noticed Charlie's arm in a cast and learned that he'd broken his wrist after he punched out a laborer who attacked him a week or two earlier."

Charlie didn't go easy on the teenager that first day. "He told me to move a big sand pile 10 feet – the job was in the masonry stage of construction. After I moved the pile in two hours, he knew he had somebody who would be a good, hard worker."

Charlie was like a lot of the J.E. Dunn superintendents of that era, according to Terry. "Many had been sergeants in the Army and Marines or petty officers in the Navy during World War II. Their motto was 'my way or the highway.' They got results."

Peer Review: The Birth of Quality Assurance

One of those men, an ironworkers' superintendent named Bill Jones, saved J.E. Dunn from making a costly mistake at one of the company's biggest projects of the mid-1960s: the building of the Vista Del Rio retirement apartments. At 19 stories high, the apartment building at the northeast corner of Cherry Street and Admiral Boulevard in downtown Kansas City was the tallest structure the construction company had yet attempted. Towering

McGee Hall at Rockhurst College, now Rockhurst University, where Terry Dunn was initiated into the construction business under Charlie Wakeman's supervision.

J.E. Dunn construction cranes – familiar sights in the Kansas City skyline today – made their first appearance on the project.

Besides being the first J.E. Dunn job to use a climbing crane, Vista Del Rio marked another important first for the construction company: "It introduced the concept of peer review," remembers Bill Dunn. Before the climbing crane even arrived at the site, Jones sensed something wrong and told Bill that the structural engineer didn't know what he was doing. Bill Dunn took the plans to another structural engineer, Bob Campbell, who wasn't at all eager to review them. "I'll get sued," Campbell said. After Bill assured him that the construction company would defend him if there were a lawsuit, Campbell reviewed the original structural engineer's design and confirmed Bill Jones' worst suspicions. For one, shear walls had been left out of the design. Without shear walls, a wind blowing at 40 to 45 miles per hour could have caused the top of the building to sway and topple over.

Campbell also found that there was not enough reinforcing steel to adequately support the parking garage on the sloping site. Bill Dunn gave the report to the building's architect, John Lawrence Daw, who fired the original structural engineer and asked Campbell to take his place.

According to Bill Dunn, peer review involves, "architects talking to us about structural issues before a job gets underway. The norm at the time was for architects to ignore the contractors' input on structural matters." Now, as part of a practice called "quality assurance," the construction company routinely hires engineers to review plans, looking for structural problems and checking soil conditions before the first shovel is turned at a site.

Nearly 40 years later, city officials may wish the architect and builder hadn't paid so much attention to structural integrity at the Vista Del Rio. For years it stood as one of the city's tallest eyesores – a concrete shell tattooed in graffiti. In July 2003, The View LLC, a development group, began renovating the building. Another retirement home built by J.E. Dunn during the 1960s, the Paraclete Manor Apartments at 4725 Prospect Avenue, had a happier fate. The 121-room apartment building has continuously served as a home for elderly people since J.E. Dunn completed it in the fall of 1966.

Schools and Training Centers

*T*hough the retirement age population in America grew during the 1960s, the young baby boom generation continued to be the focus of many J.E. Dunn projects.

In February 1967, J.E. Dunn submitted the winning bid for building Franklin Elementary, a public school for 1,200 students at 35th Street and Wayne Avenue in Kansas City. The next month it was low bidder on an unnamed public junior high and elementary school at 43rd and Indiana. After Martin Luther King Jr. was killed that spring, it was decided that the junior and elementary schools would be named in his honor.

In September 1968, J.E. Dunn crews returned to Manual High School, the vocational-technical school where the construction company had worked before the World War II era. Construction on the Manual site was planned in two phases over a two-year period. During the first phase, a new school would be built around the old one where the currently enrolled students would finish out the 1968-69 school year. Next, parts of the old Manual would be razed while other sections would be incorporated into the new building. No one looking at the windowless exterior of the new five-story building would recognize old Manual High School when the project was completed.

While J.E. Dunn built elementary, junior high, and high schools in Kansas City, it continued to change the face of the campus at Central Missouri State College in Warrensburg throughout the 1960s.

J.E. Dunn would no sooner complete one college project when the company would submit the winning bid for another big construction job on the Warrensburg campus. During the decade, J.E. Dunn built two men's dormitories, a women's dormitory, the college library, the language and literature building, the education building, and a power and technology center at the college. When additions were made to the dormitories and the library, the construction company did that work as well, with Bill Miller acting as J.E. Dunn superintendent. J.E. Dunn also built three apartment complexes for students just south of the campus.

College students weren't the only young adults in search of classrooms and housing in the 1960s in the Midwest; young women who wanted to become flight attendants were also in the market. Trans World Airlines found a place for their training at the northern edge of Overland Park, Kan., just outside of Kansas City. "On this 34-acre site will rise the most modern education complex in the world of aviation," declared Mr. R.M. Dunn, TWA senior vice president and system general manager, in the June 1968 edition of *Modern Builder*. Dunn, no relation to anyone at the construction company, wasn't exaggerating: the TWA Breech Academy would have all "the bells

Manual Technical School after J.E. Dunn modernized its appearance.

and whistles" a flight attendant in training could hope for.

Plans called for a two-level administrative training building that had aircraft cabins, emergency trainers, and galleys to simulate actual working conditions aboard the firm's aircraft. Included was a 61-foot, three-section trainer for the Boeing 747, the giant commercial jetliner that TWA expected to put into service in early 1970. This trainer and the others – a Boeing

707, 727 and Douglas DC-9 – were designed to scale and would be housed in specially built rooms. There would be 30 classrooms on the complex, an auditorium with a seating capacity for 300, a 30-chair beauty salon, three residential buildings for housing 600 trainees, and a swimming pool enclosed under a dome for year-round use. It

A conference room at the Waddell & Reed Investment Company office park. J.E. Dunn built the TWA Breech Academy at the site in the late 1960s and returned in the early 1990s to convert it into headquarters for the investment company.

Building will be inside only."[9] Historic preservationists in Kansas City finally had something to cheer about: the exterior of the old building remained unchanged. The same couldn't be said for the construction industry in Kansas City that year – 1969 would usher in drastic changes.

would be the ultimate flight attendant factory – just as one group of young women completed their training over a six-and-a-half week period, the academy would welcome the next batch of trainees. Two thousand flight attendants would be trained each year.

J.E. Dunn set TWA's plans in motion, beating out several other bidders on the $10 million job in the spring of 1968. The complex became known as the TWA Breech Academy, named after Ernest R. Breech, chairman emeritus of the TWA board of directors. The construction company would return to the site in the early 1990s to convert the former training academy into an office park for Waddell & Reed Investment Company. The main training facility for flight attendants became the company headquarters for Waddell & Reed and the three former dormitories

were converted into office suites for the investment company's business tenants.

Not all of the Dunn projects during the 1960s involved new construction. In 1965 the construction company did remodeling work for H.O. Peet & Co., the stock brokerage firm, at its ground floor offices in the Insurance Exchange Building at the southeast corner of 10th and Baltimore in downtown Kansas City. Two years later it began remodeling the interior of the brokerage firm's offices at 4725 Wyandotte on the Plaza. The owner of the Insurance Exchange Building and a longtime client of J.E. Dunn, the J.A. Bruening Co., selected the construction company to gut and rebuild the rest of the 16-story granite and brick structure in downtown Kansas City in 1969. A caption in the Kansas City Star read, "The new look for the Insurance Exchange

Labor Strikes Back

*I*t seems appropriate that the strike of 3,000 area construction industry workers would share front-page headlines with funeral arrangements for former U.S. President Dwight D. Eisenhower in the April 1, 1969 edition of *The Kansas City Times*. If Kansas Citians had any doubt that the "business as usual" attitude of the Eisenhower era was long gone, reports on the strike should have convinced them. At midnight on that day, workers from three local unions went on strike: painters from District Council No. 3, ironworkers from Local No. 10, and lumberyard workers and drivers from Teamsters Local No. 541.

Representatives of the painters and ironworkers faced off with management, represented by the Builders' Association, on the issue of wages, fringe benefits, and working conditions. The lumberyard workers and drivers were involved in a separate wage dispute with the local Lumber Dealers Association. They were all part of a nationwide trend. Across the country, about 1.4 million workers won wage increases of more than 7 percent in the first half of 1969, according to the U.S. Labor Department.[10] Large wage settlements in the construction industry, averaging about 15 percent a year, raised the overall average.

In the early days of the strike, it didn't look like management would budge. "They wouldn't even negotiate," Bill Richardson, the painters' representative complained. "We gave them a new proposal that was scaled down in wages, but they just didn't seem to want to talk." Management's representative, W.W. "Bill" Hutton, managing director of the Builders' Association, explained his position, "The painters and ironworkers are asking for an 80 percent increase in the cost of labor. If this kind of increase were extended to other trades, construction costs in Kansas City would jump 40 percent overnight."[11]

Painters and ironworkers responded by setting up picket lines at many area projects including one of J.E. Dunn's biggest jobs at the time, the TWA Breech Academy. In fact, a much wider shutdown loomed; a prolonged strike of ironworkers eventually could tie up jobs where there were no pickets because ironwork had to be finished before other crafts could proceed. "Greater Kansas City stands on the brink of a labor-management crisis that could stop the current construction boom for an indefinite period," warned an editorial writer for the *Kansas City Times* on April 2.

J.E. Dunn was poised to become part of the construction boom that spring. The construction company beat out four other bidders in April to build an eight-story hospital for the Kansas City College of Osteopathic Medicine. The new hospital would replace the old 100-bed Osteopathic Hospital and the Conley Maternity Hospital, both at 11th and Harrison. It would be built about two blocks west of the college's main building at 2015 Independence Avenue.

Unfortunately, the directors of the hospital could hardly have picked a worse time to sign a construction contract. The strike spread to a fourth construction trade, the sheet metal workers, on July 1. Strikes delayed the groundbreaking until July 11, 1969. Labor problems continued to plague the job and many other large construction projects of the era.

As the strikes stretched into summer, several local government officials and federal mediators tried to help the labor negotiations along. The painters were the first to break the standoff, signing a new contract on July 13 that gave them a $3.18 an hour wage increase over a three-year period. By April 1971, their base would be $7.92 an hour.

For about two weeks, the painters could boast the largest single increase in Kansas City construction labor history.[12] Then the ironworkers broke their record on July 28, by ratifying a contract that raised their hourly wages from $5.00 to $9.05.[13]

The strikes of 1969 gave Kansas City the dubious distinction of leading the nation in total number of man-days lost due to strikes. Second place in 1969 went to St. Louis. It had more work stoppages, involving more workers, but its strikes lasted a shorter period of time. The state of Missouri topped all states in 1969, with more than five million man-days rendered idle by strikes.

Despite the wage boosts, Kansas City still lagged behind the rest of the country

ECONOMIC CRISIS!

K.C. Star - May 12, 1970

AN OPEN LETTER TO THE LABORERS OF KANSAS CITY

Do the members of Locals 1290, 264, 555 and 663 want to be known as the men who stopped the building boom in Kansas City— the men who wrecked the bright promise of prosperity for all?

The Builder's Association does not believe this is so. We want the rank-and-file to understand the issues involved.

The union demand for a four dollar per hour increase in 1970, and a total of six dollars an hour *increase* over three years, cannot be met without crippling the building industry. We have offered three dollars an hour *increase* over three years.

It is true that the International Airport and the Sports Complex will provide many jobs over the next two years; but, beyond that, there are no other major projects of this magnitude to sustain this level of employment.

In the area of private construction, 110 projects representing 288 million dollars have been completely dropped following the 1969 Iron Workers/Painters wage settlement. Not enough new projects are being started to suport the area trades in the immediate years ahead. This continuing

"Striking construction workers are stopping the local building boom," complains a writer from the Builders' Association of Greater Kansas City in the spring of 1970.

in some hourly wage scales. For example, the new wages that local painters had bargained for and won were still 21 cents below the national average.[14] Area carpenters earned $5.00 an hour compared to the national average of $5.84. Labor and management had merely called a truce when the ironworkers' strike was settled; the local battle was far from over.

Once the ironworkers were back at work, most of the commercial construction projects could resume even though the lumberyard workers remained on strike. While catching up with ongoing projects, J.E. Dunn continued to find new work. In August 1969, the construction company won another hospital, an unnamed extended care facility that would be built between 25th and 26th Streets and Garfield and Euclid Avenues. Later named the Martin Luther King, Jr., Memorial Hospital, the 126-bed, six-story building would be built from a precast concrete frame and insulated glass. Financing for the project depended largely on grant money from the Department of Housing and Urban Development. The times being what they were, it did not take long for government red tape and labor strikes to hobble the project.

Though the J.E. Dunn crews stayed busy when they were not idled by strikes, the construction company missed out on some of Kansas City's biggest projects of the era – Kansas City International Airport, the Harry S. Truman Sports Complex, and Hallmark's Crown Center Development. J.E. Dunn hadn't yet broken into the market of "mega-jobs."

During the latter half of 1969 and through early 1970, the construction boom seemed to be back on track. Unfortunately, it all screeched to a halt on April 1, 1970, with the strike of five unions: the two Laborers' Locals No. 264 and 1290, Mason and Plaster Tenders Union Local No. 555, Cement Finishers Union Local No. 518, and Lathers Union Local No. 27. This time, some 5,000 construction laborers walked off their jobs, but with the additional workers affected, the total number of workers out of jobs because of the strike exceeded 20,000. Within a week, strikers put up pickets at several jobs where they accused nonstriking workers of performing their work.

While local politicians and business owners complained, people involved in the construction industry had a more immediate concern: finding work during the strike. "J.E. Dunn kept all of its office people employed," Ardyth Wendte recalls. Ardyth remembers how her own work assignment changed. "There wasn't much for me to do in the office once billings had fallen off to almost nothing, so Ernie and Bill thought it would be the ideal time for their mother, Rose Dunn, to write a personal history of her family and the beginnings of the construction company. I would take notes as she recalled past events. The notes evolved into a small booklet that she gave to her family and friends."

Field employees had a harder time. Some had to travel as far away as St. Louis to find work. Others just waited.

Finally, on October 13, Albert H. Meinert, international vice president of Plasterers and Cement Masons of the United States and Canada, reached an agreement with the Builders' Association. The agreement was not subject to approval by the union membership; it essentially ended the city's almost six-and-a-half month construction strike. Members of three locals still were without contracts, Lathers Local No. 27 and ready-mix concrete workers belonging to Locals No. 663 and 1290, but they did not delay the return to work. For his part, Bill Hutton at the Builders' Association was not thrilled with the agreement, which called for the cement masons to receive a $4.57 per half hour pay hike over four years. "I still think the settlement was inflationary, but there comes a time when we have to go back

Minorities Make Broad Inroads into Construction

*W*hile organized labor and management were thrashing things out between themselves in the late 1960s and early 1970s, representatives of the civil rights movement attacked both sides for excluding minorities from the ranks of the local construction industry. In February 1970, Kansas City was among 19 cities targeted by the U.S. Department of Labor as needing voluntary plans for including minority groups in union membership. Construction trades in Kansas City, as in most other cities, had low percentages of minorities in union membership. The ironworkers, electricians, and plumbers came under especial criticism for excluding minority group members. The Ironworkers Union Local No. 10 said it had one black journeyman and a few apprentices out of about 1,200 members. Plumbers Union Local No. 8 had seven black journeymen and seven black apprentices out of about 865 working members. Electricians Local No. 124 did not have figures available to report to the

Kansas City Times about the number of blacks among its 1,600 members.[15]

Ernie Jr. spearheaded an effort to settle the dispute when he and William J. Stack, secretary-manager of the labor union council, agreed to head a local committee to prepare a plan for integrating the construction industry. Black leaders such as Dr. Vernon Rice, head of the local chapter of the NAACP, soon demanded a role in the planning. "We are dubious that this group of builders and union officials alone will develop an acceptable plan for the future inclusion of minorities in the construction crafts. We shall oppose any plan developed without substantial participation [by blacks]," Rice stated in a telegram.[16]

"I would imagine that we will plan to bring in as many representatives of every group involved in this problem to produce a plan fair to all persons," Ernie replied. He led a nine-man committee made up of three representatives of management, three representatives from labor, and three minority members. They eventually hammered out an agreement in August 1970, and drafters of the agreement predicted it would put 1,100 additional minority workers on local construction jobs within five years.

Ernie sounded a cautionary note on the plan's effectiveness: "No plan can work – whether it is legally binding or not – if

to work, and under these circumstances it was time to compromise."

Despite the best of planning, surprises are always possible at a job site.

Martin Luther King Jr. Hospital was completed early in 1972, but not before the J.E. Dunn workers dug up a little forgotten Kansas City history. "Old Burial Ground at Martin Luther King Haunting Workers," read the headline for the story in the Oct. 6, 1971 *Kansas City Star*. Buford House, J.E. Dunn superintendent on the job, guessed that construction workers had unearthed as many as 50 graves. The site was the location for the old Saints Peter and Paul Catholic Cemetery until it closed in 1923. An official with the city health department insisted that all the bodies had been moved to another cemetery years before. The construction crew begged to differ. "Ain't none of 'em been moved, pardner," said one construction worker. "I've dug up too many myself." The crews wasted little time in reburying the remains where they found them.

Twenty years later, the same thing happened when the coffins of early French settlers were unearthed during the excavation of the Hereford Building on the west side of Kansas City. Once again, church records showed the bodies had been relocated many years before, and once again workers proved that "official" records can't always be trusted.

Martin Luther King Jr. Memorial Hospital stood on the site of an old cemetery.

the people involved don't intend to make it work." He added, "We intend to make it work."[17]

The city of Kansas City did its part to integrate the construction industry in July 1973 by passing an ordinance requiring businesses to show that they were equal opportunity employers.[18] To obtain a city certificate, a bidder had to submit existing employment records showing a plan for equal opportunity employment for the previous 12 months. The records had to show the number of minorities and women employed and the business had to describe and justify its recruiting methods. Now, more than 30 years later,

(above) L-R: Steve, Terry, and Bill Dunn Jr. at Terry's graduation from Rockhurst College in May 1971. That summer Steve got his first taste of the construction business, working as a laborer on the Osteopathic Hospital site.

(left) The framework of a new building at Penn Valley Community College is cast in silhouette by the setting sun.

minorities play a larger role in Kansas City's construction field than they once did. Unfortunately, their struggle for equal opportunity is far from over.

Work After the Strikes

*B*y late fall of 1970, idled bulldozers began chugging at construction sites again, concrete began flowing through pumps once more, and construction foremen barked out directions to their workers the way they had before the strikes. J.E. Dunn was finally able to finish some of the projects it had begun before the strikes, such as the Brothers of Mercy Extended Care Hospital at 22nd and Charlotte in the Hospital Hill area. The 126-bed extended care facility was completed in January 1971, three months after the strike ended.

Steve Dunn remembers another strike-delayed project only too well. As an 18-year-old just completing his freshman year at Rockhurst College, Steve was one of the youngest laborers working at the Osteopathic Hospital site during the summer of 1971. He remembers working for labor foremen Everett Reynolds and Larry Jackson. The $29 million teaching hospital, originally scheduled to finish in mid-1971, didn't wrap up until late 1972.

Penn Valley Community College was remarkable for its tight construction

schedule. Like many clients who had to wait out the two long strikes, the Metropolitan Junior College district officials were anxious to speed the work along once the strikes were over. College officials took a cue from other progressive owners by putting a "critical path scheduling" plan into their contracts with the architect and the builder. Critical path scheduling was a new idea in the 1970s, relying on computers to determine the most efficient time sequence on a construction project by revealing how best to coordinate the efforts of the different crafts on a job.

As part of the plan, the college hired Langston Kitch & Associates Inc., a project management/consulting firm, to work with J.E. Dunn to schedule the timing and sequence of tasks on the job. Bill Dunn had worked with scheduling consultants on other projects, but none impressed him more than Lou Hilker from Langston Kitch. "Lou was the first consultant in critical path scheduling that I met who really knew how to put the various pieces of a job together." Under the direction of Lou Hilker and project superintendent Bill Miller, the job was completed by the winter of 1973.

Lou Hilker's skills in critical path scheduling have helped J.E. Dunn meet many construction deadlines.

Effects of the Strikes

While innovations like critical path scheduling helped the construction company finish older jobs, J.E. Dunn broke ground on new work soon after the 1970 strike. New projects included an eight-story addition to the Southwestern Bell Telephone Building at 1425 Oak in downtown Kansas City, the Jackson County Juvenile Detention Center at 27th and Cherry, and Temple Heights Manor, a nine-story apartment building for the elderly at 55th and Blue Ridge Cutoff in Raytown, Mo. In Kansas, J.E. Dunn started construction on the Beal office building in Overland Park and the Woodside Racquet Club in Westwood while it finished work at the TWA Breech Academy. The health care building boom of the 1960s began to pick up again for J.E. Dunn in the early 1970s, with a steady stream of projects: the new Liberty Hospital, a $17 million addition to Menorah Medical Center, and a five-story medical office building next to North Kansas City Memorial Hospital. Yet another job would prove to be a breakthrough project for J.E. Dunn – construction of the $30 million Truman Medical Center on Hospital Hill in Kansas City.

It may have looked like the same old construction industry, but things had changed since the strike. Miller Nichols, president of the J.C. Nichols Company, had predicted during the strike that Kansas City's hostile labor market would have outside investors looking elsewhere for their new buildings. His prediction came true according to Bill Dunn: "Many national companies with building projects stayed away from the region for the next 10 years."

The higher labor wages resulting from strike settlements had a more immediate effect on owners already building in the area: significantly higher project costs. "With wages doubling in a two to three year period, owners and architects were having a terrible time trying to figure out what their budgets should be," Bill Dunn remembers. "Before the strikes of 1969 and 1970, owners and architects rarely talked to contractors about budget matters. After the strikes, they were often forced to."

Partially as a result of the new pressure on budgets, the era of negotiated construction projects was beginning in Kansas City, and J.E. Dunn had the expertise to be a participant. "From the 1970s onward, a great deal of our work has been negotiated," Bill says.

A new vocabulary evolved to describe how large contractors like J.E. Dunn could help owners and architects keep building costs down. "Critical path scheduling," "fast track construction," and "value engineering" became the construction buzz phrases of the day. J.E. Dunn marketed them as team concepts involving the architect, owner, and itself – the general contractor.

Fast track construction and critical path scheduling represented two approaches to cutting down the time from a construction project's inception to its completion, thereby saving owners money. Fast track construction allowed construction to begin before the architect's drawings were completed and thus saved time and money during the earlier phases of a project. It was often the best alternative for an owner faced with a tight schedule. The challenge for the contractor in fast track construction was to determine guaranteed building costs based on incomplete drawings. J.E. Dunn's experience helped it make those cost determinations.

Where fast track construction might get a project started sooner, critical path scheduling would speed things along

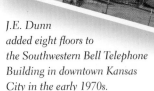

J.E. Dunn added eight floors to the Southwestern Bell Telephone Building in downtown Kansas City in the early 1970s.

The Liberty Hospital.

from the groundbreaking to a building's completion. Long before the term "value engineering" was coined, J.E. Dunn was already advising owners and architects on ways to hold down costs during construction. The role of the contractor in value engineering was to present the owner and architect with alternative methods or materials to reduce the cost of a project without sacrificing quality. After the strike settlements of 1969 and 1970 had boosted construction costs to new highs, more architects and owners were willing to listen to J.E. Dunn's cost-cutting alternatives.

In time, some owners were willing to forego the competitive bidding process to get J.E. Dunn as their contractor. Some owners and architects would even come to think of themselves as "team players" with J.E. Dunn on certain projects. No one would have predicted that outcome before the strikes.

On the other hand, it would be years before members of labor and management felt like they played on the same team.

The Kemper Arena's design drew favorable reviews from the American Institute of Architects.

Labor-management relations remained strained after the 1970 strike settled. The Kemper Arena project would highlight both the new alliance between owners, architects, and contractors and the lingering tensions between builders and union workers.

The Kemper Arena

*I*n the world of professional sports, competition between cities for a franchise can get as heated as emotions between opposing athletes at a play-off game. Kansas City found itself in a race in the early 1970s, vying to get a team in the National Hockey League. To be a contender in this race, the city would have to provide an arena seating 16,000 to 18,000 people and have it ready for occupancy for the 1974-75 season. Family members of the late banking leader R. Crosby Kemper Sr., gave the city an edge in the competition when they donated $2.5 million for an arena where both the hockey team and the American Royal, a sponsor of indoor horse shows and rodeo events, would be the prime tenants. Supporters of the American Royal donated another $1.2 million to have the arena built on land in Kansas City's West Bottoms, where the stockyards used to be. In late December 1972, a panel made up of city officials and American Royal board members chose C.F. Murphy

and Associates, a Chicago architecture firm, to design the arena.

Instead of submitting a firm bid price to the owner at the onset, J.E. Dunn offered a maximum price to erect the design/build project. Before construction began, J.E. Dunn worked closely with the architect to cost-design the project in just 27 days, and fast track construction allowed J.E. Dunn to break ground in June 1973, long before the architect's detailed work drawings were complete. J.E. Dunn offered its value engineering advice to the architect, allowing C.F. Murphy to choose a concept that was both aesthetic and economical. With the overview of critical path scheduling, the project seemed to be breezing along until a few snags appeared.

The first major delay came when workers at the Kansas City Structural Steel Company, a major materials supplier for the job, decided to strike, followed on May 6, 1974, by bricklayers from Local Unions 4 and 18. The arena was one of 16 construction sites where they picketed. Just as it began to look like a flashback to the 1969 and 1970 strikes, something curious happened – other crafts began crossing the bricklayers' picket lines within a month after the strike began. Roofers were among the first to cross the picket lines. By mid-June, other crafts announced

Worlds of Fun.

their intention to cross the pickets. Union sources said that 10 trades that had settled for 8 percent wage increases earlier that spring were disgruntled that the bricklayers were demanding higher increases, according to the June 13, 1974 edition of *The Kansas City Star.* Bricklayers contended that they had dropped to 13th in wages among other unions and deserved to be on an equal footing with the other crafts. Builders and the bricklayers reached an agreement on June 15.

Returning to work after the bricklayers strike, J.E. Dunn workers were determined to put the arena building back on schedule. "If anybody sees smoke rising from the bottoms, it's this job going full blast," General Superintendent Woody Randolph told reporters.[19] The Kemper Arena was ready November 2 for the opening game of the Kansas City Scouts hockey team. J.E. Dunn had completed the project on time for $29,860 below the guaranteed maximum price. Glen J. Hopkins, deputy city manager, praised the construction company: "It is a real tribute to Bill Dunn that he held down the price and completed the arena in 17 months despite being shut down for three months by strikes."[20]

In 1976, The American Institute of Architects named the arena as one of 10 winners of its annual honor awards.

The jury of architects described the arena as a "coliseum turned inside out with its structural supports exposed." The jury admired the giant trusses that spanned above the arena roof combined with the subtly articulated metal siding on the building's exterior: "[It] makes an elegant architectural statement rarely found in this building type."[21] The Kemper Arena seemed to be a victory for everyone involved in its design and construction. Unfortunately, events a few years later would turn the praise into accusations.

On June 4, 1979, a violent storm with high winds and torrential rain swept through the city around dinnertime. Kemper Arena was collecting as much as a foot of water on its flat roof because of an inadequate drainage system. J.E. Dunn had sought second opinions on a number of structural issues during the construction, but the potential drainage problem was not caught. When the pipes failed to siphon off enough water, the tons of extra weight collapsed the roof. Fortunately, the building was empty and no one was hurt. Though not at fault, everyone at J.E. Dunn was devastated by the collapse. Taking on the repair without profit, they had the building operational again within six months.

Worlds of Fun

*T*ight construction schedules were becoming the rule rather than the exception for J.E. Dunn in the early 1970s with projects like the Kemper Arena and an even bigger rush job, Worlds of Fun in Kansas City. When J.E. Dunn signed on to build the 140-acre amusement park in May 1972, it agreed to complete the project by the following spring. Bill Dunn remembers the budget being as tight as the schedule. "We bid the job competitively and were low bidder, but our price still exceeded their budget." He suggested certain changes to reduce costs. The owners agreed to a guaranteed cost and promised to return any savings on the job back to the contractor. Lamar Hunt, owner of the Kansas City Chiefs and Worlds of Fun chairman, expressed approval in bringing the construction company on board. "The J.E. Dunn Construction Company has a reputation for quality work," he said.[22]

The work would include the construction of 60 buildings, at least 20 special rides, and recreational features such as a railroad, an amphitheater, and three lakes, each holding a ship featured in a Hollywood movie. In the same newspaper article where Lamar Hunt was quoted, Jack Steadman, president of Worlds of Fun, described the volume of material that would be used on the project: 22 boxcar loads of lumber, three miles of plumbing, 2.5 acres of roofing material and 35 miles of electric wiring would be needed to create the five international areas in the park. About 15,000 tons of concrete materials, 25,000 tons of crushed rock and 34,000 cubic yards of asphalt would be needed to build the 5,000 car parking area and the many miles of asphalt walkways and building foundations.

Worlds of Fun was hardly going to be a run-of-the-mill project for the construction company. Bill Dunn knew it would take an all-out effort to finish a job of that scale in only a year's time. To push the project along, he recommended the owners use the critical path scheduling skills of Lou Hilker, who was still working for Langston Kitch at the time. Bill told Lamar Hunt and

Jack Steadman how Lou's scheduling had sped work along in building the Penn Valley campus. Bill also recalled how rain and snow threatened to slow things down once the work started: "The weather was the worst but the superintendent, Charlie Wakeman, kept

driving and driving until the project was finished. He did a great job."

The job went so well, in fact, that when it was over J.E. Dunn was entitled to $100,000 in savings from the owner. Rather than collect the savings, Bill Dunn returned the money to Jack Steadman,

(l-r) Jack Steadman, president of Worlds of Fun; Stan McIlvaine, general manager at Worlds of Fun; and Bill Dunn Sr. watch Chiefs owner and Worlds of Fun chairman Lamar Hunt sign on the dotted line.

telling him, "This job has been a real experience for us and as far as I'm concerned, you might as well negotiate that out of our contract. We may be entitled to it but it's been a good job for us."

The owners were shocked. "The contrast between J.E. Dunn and another contractor that we'd just worked with was a real eye-opener," says Jack Steadman. "We'd had some difficulty with the other contractor on the fairness of his costs. In contrast, it was always an honest relationship with Bill Dunn. The Dunn philosophy is to give you a quality product at a fair price."

The Brothers Go Their Separate Ways

*T*he Worlds of Fun owners weren't the only ones shocked when Bill returned $100,000 in savings to them. It also drew a strong response from Ernie Jr. "It was the straw that broke the camel's back in my business relationship with my brother," Bill says in hindsight. In many ways, Ernie's reaction was understandable: it was virtually unprecedented for a construction company to give $100,000 back to an owner – money to which J.E. Dunn was clearly entitled.

Bill defends the decision. "I thought we already made a fair fee on the project."

Business relations had grown strained between the brothers long before the Worlds of Fun contract was ever signed. For one, it bothered Bill that business administration procedures at J.E. Dunn were not keeping pace with its growing field operations and bigger revenues. He felt the larger size of the company demanded an update in how the business was run. Ernie, on the other hand, didn't see the need for the internal changes, perhaps because he was not as directly involved in the field operations. His duties managing J.E. Dunn's real estate holdings, serving as president of the Associated General Contractors in the early 1970s, and other civic roles were demanding a larger share of his time. With their different job responsibilities, the brothers spent less time working together. The gap between their business philosophies was widening.

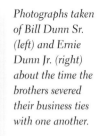

Photographs taken of Bill Dunn Sr. (left) and Ernie Dunn Jr. (right) about the time the brothers severed their business ties with one another.

In 1973, both Ernie and Bill hired their own attorneys to figure the best way for one brother to buy out the other's interest in J.E. Dunn. Bill turned to Jim Seigfreid, a lawyer who had a formidable reputation representing Lamar Hunt's organization. Seigfreid referred him to a young lawyer in his firm, Larry Bingham.

Larry Bingham remembers the dilemma facing the brothers. "Both Ernie and Bill wanted to run the company, so it's not like we had a buyer and a seller, which is easier to negotiate." A sticking point for both brothers was in figuring out how much the company was worth.

Bill credits Larry with an idea that helped break the impasse. "Larry saw that there were really two companies involved: Dunleith Towers Properties, which represented all the real estate interests, and J.E. Dunn, the company actually involved in the construction business." Bill says, "I put a very low price on the real estate because I wasn't interested in it and I probably put too high a price on the construction company."

Larry and Bill presented a purchase offer to Ernie and his lawyer, Gene Mitchell. "Some people would call our proposal an 'Arkansas Choice,'" Larry recalls. "Bill was either going to be a buyer or seller for this price and let Ernie make the choice." The proposal made no limitations on competition. The brother who sold his share in J.E. Dunn would be free to start his own construction company. After months of negotiations, Ernie agreed to sell his family's share in the company in February 1974. Bill would have five years to pay off the obligation.

Larry looks back on the significance of that period. "Setting the purchase price was the most important thing Bill did in his career. I think his optimism had a lot to do with it – he thought about what he could do with the company, not what it was doing then, because he would run it differently."

Bill's optimism turned out to be well-founded. It wouldn't be easy to pay off his debt to Ernie's family, but his own hard work, coupled with the dedicated efforts of the J.E. Dunn employees who remained, proved they were all up to the challenge.

After selling his share in J.E. Dunn and the real estate holdings, Ernie began his own construction company, J.E. Dunn Jr. and Associates. Cy Young and Beverly Kidder Snyder, who had worked at J.E. Dunn in the office, went to work at Ernie's newly formed company along with several J.E. Dunn superintendents. A few of Ernie's sons also joined the new construction company, which met with much success in the years that followed.

Now that Ernie is retired, one of his sons, Tom, carries on the family tradition, running his own Kansas City business, K C Heritage Construction Company. Fortunately, the business split didn't taint the relationship between the two brothers, Bill and Ernie, who remain close to this day. Both are relieved that the difficult years are behind them.

One of the toughest years for the brothers and their sisters, Mary Ellen and Rosalie, was 1974. Their mother, Rose Dunn died that May at the age of 78. Her condition had grown steadily worse after she had fallen on some ice and broken a hip two years earlier. The time she spent bedridden in pain took a toll on her emotionally. Death may have come as a blessing for Rose, but it left a void for her children and grandchildren. Rose had been the glue that held the family together, even while her husband was alive. Now she was gone.

Chapter 4
THE SURVIVAL YEARS
1974-1980

Building No.12 at Corporate Woods.

THE 1970S

Turmoil

As 1974 dawned in America, social change and turmoil continued to be the order of the day.

*T*he previous year, *Roe vs. Wade* had legalized abortion, establishing a beachhead of controversy that would rage for decades. Native Americans had recaptured the small hamlet of Wounded Knee, S. D., asserting the presence and rights of yet another minority. In October 1973, Vice President Spiro Agnew had resigned after a federal grand jury began hearing charges that he had participated in widespread graft as an officeholder in Maryland. He was replaced by Gerald Ford, a respected Michigan congressman who was virtually unknown to all but the most astute political observers. President Nixon himself was caught in the midst of the Watergate affair that would soon drive him from office, and the energy crisis was driving gas prices ever higher, creating long lines at the pump.

For the establishment, the world had been constantly shifting since the 1960s,

Bill Dunn Sr. faced the same sorts of financial challenges in construction during the1970s that his father had dealt with in an earlier era.

but not all the changes were negative. By February 1974, several technological advances were making themselves known. Skylab, America's first space station, had been launched, Stephen Jobs was already developing a home computer in his California garage, and Dr. Christiaan Barnard, a coronary surgeon in South Africa, had performed the world's first heart transplant.

Unfortunately, the country was wrestling with both the worst economic slump of the past forty years and soaring interest rates, but significant construction projects were nevertheless underway. The world's tallest building, the Sears Tower in Chicago, and I.M. Pei's east wing of the National Gallery in Washington, D.C., were about to break ground.

Kansas City, under Mayor Charles Wheeler, continued to grow with the rest of the nation, annexing large tracts of land in all directions. New additions to the cityscape included the Harry S. Truman Sports Complex, boasting Arrowhead and Royals stadiums, and the massive new Kansas City International Airport.

At the J.E. Dunn offices in downtown Kansas City, challenge and opportunity were both plentiful. After the buyout, the company had a negative net worth of $1.1 million, a daunting figure at any time, but particularly frightening during a recession. With the consumer price index on its way to a 126 percent rise between 1970 and 1980, and the cost of construction rocketing over 150 percent

WHAT'S DUNN DOING?

We're utilizing our 50 years expertise in the building construction industry and combining it with modern methods of Cost Design, Fast Track and Critical Path Scheduling. These tools enable us to complete our client's project on schedule and within the budget. Our new symbol, like all hallmarks of fine craftsmanship, signifies our commitment to excellence.

J. E. DUNN CONSTRUCTION CO.
929 HOLMES · KANSAS CITY, MISSOURI · 474-8600
Since 1924
An Equal Opportunity Employer

A J.E. Dunn logo appeared in the mid-1970s.

The Holiday Inn near the Kansas City Chiefs and Royals stadiums was one of four hotels facing money problems during its construction in 1974.

Even though J.E. Dunn had plenty of work underway, Bill Dunn was concerned in 1974 because of the debt owed to his brother and because the owners at four hotel projects – two Holiday Inns, a Ramada Inn, and a Rodeway Inn – were all having financial difficulties. It was a lucky break for J.E. Dunn when the lending bank took over the two Holiday Inns and paid for their construction.

The owners of the other two hotels finally worked out their problems, and months after their final payments were due, they paid the construction company.

during the same period, potential clients were very careful about committing to new construction. "All of us knew we were in a survival mode," says Bill. "We had five years to pay off the debt."

But Bill had a number of things going for him. First, J.E. Dunn Construction was well-known and well-respected in Kansas City, one of a number of the city's sizable contractors, along with Universal Construction Company, Bennett, Winn-Senter, Eldridge, Sharp, and DiCarlo. Second, they had just completed several major projects, including the Johnson County (Kan.) Courthouse addition and the high-profile Worlds of Fun

Amusement Park for Lamar Hunt's Midwest Enterprises.

These projects helped pave the way for the future. By returning $100,000 to the owners, Bill handled the Worlds of Fun project in a way that was reminiscent of his father's dealings with the Quartermaster Depot during World War II. Ernie Sr. had also refused profits. The results were the same in both circumstances – J.E. Dunn Construction Company earned respect and, Bill believes, excellent publicity. "Lamar Hunt and Jack Steadman probably provided us marketing opportunities that we would have never been able to get in the rest of the community here, so [the $100,000] probably came back many times over," Bill muses.

Re-tooling for the Future

$\mathcal{P}$artially as a result of the visibility and good will from the Worlds of Fun project, J.E. Dunn had a number of substantial jobs underway when Bill bought the company from Ernie – the Liberty District Hospital, Kemper Arena, a couple of office buildings and church projects, and four hotels: the Ramada Inn near KCI Airport, the Holiday Inn near KCI Airport, the Holiday Inn near the Harry S. Truman Sports Complex, and the Rodeway Inn in Grandview. J.E. Dunn had also bought from Ernie a significant amount of real estate in various locations around Kansas City and three apartment complexes in Warrensburg, Mo.

Bill Dunn counted his people among his greatest assets. "I think if you're looking at why we've been able to stick around," he says today, "particularly for what I figure were the survival years after 1974, it's really people – very talented people."

In his own office, Bill counted most heavily on longtime assistant Ardyth Wendte and the more recently hired Billie Hestand. Bernard Jacquinot and Gene Payne, both already with the company over twenty years, were the veteran project managers. Fred Shipman, who began working with J.E. Dunn as a trainee under Bernard in the early 1970s, would soon become a project manager himself.

In the field, the new owner looked to the company's top superintendents – Charlie Wakeman, Bill Miller, Woody Randolph, Jack McCollom, Harry Foster, Elmer Bishop, John Spencer, and Dick Neumann. Son Terry had just joined the company to work in administration. Other critical employees, including sons Steve and Bill Jr., would begin a year later, in March of 1975, but at the time of the buyout, the crew was very small.

The company was small enough that "from the early 1970s, J.E. Dunn always provided lunch for its employees, as it still does today," recalls Ardyth Wendte. "Because there was nowhere within walking distance to eat, an experienced cook prepared food in her home and brought it to our lunchroom. If the weather was unsafe or the cook was ill, Ray Long, billings department manager, and I would go out and buy some pizza or Kentucky Fried Chicken for everyone. Our lunchroom soon became a favorite of many of our business associates whose

Superintendents who remained with J.E. Dunn Construction Company after the buyout included: Seated (l-r) John Spencer, Dick Neumann, and Woody Randolph; Standing (l-r) Jack McCollom, Charlie Wakeman, Bill Miller with Bill Dunn Sr. standing far right.

meetings sometimes carried them through the lunch hour."

From a business standpoint, the small staff had only the basic office equipment. "There were one or two electric typewriters, a few adding machines, plus a copy machine, although they were quite different from what is in use today," Ardyth says.

Filing was equally simple. "Originally, when I first started, no one really had control of the files," claims Billie Hestand. "The receptionist at that time would file when she had time and the phones weren't ringing. Old projects were boxed up and stored in the warehouse on Cherry… Once Ardyth was made corporate secretary and I was made assistant corporate secretary, Bill Dunn Sr. told us that our duties would include keeping track of the project records and corporate records for the company. From time to time, we would go out to the warehouse to file. The boxes were stacked to the ceiling on shelves, and mainly I climbed up them to file. We would get the boxes ready and log them in a book."

According to Ray Atkeisson, purchasing department manager, equipment tracking was equally primitive. "When I started in 1976, we originally used a big shoebox of index cards to track our equipment rentals. Each time

The J.E. Dunn office people in 1974 after the buyout included: Seated (l-r) Dale Shikles, Ray Long, Bernard Jacquinot, and Terry Dunn; Standing (l-r) Arnold Dreyer, Bill Dunn Sr., Gene Payne, Ardyth Wendte, Fred Shipman, and Terry Reardon.

an item of equipment was moved, you would have to pull out an index card and fill it out. At the end of the month, you'd have to review all of these index cards and charge the job."

The Point of the Lance

*B*ill Dunn's most important weapon in updating these office systems and procedures had actually been acquired before the buyout.

"About five or six months before I bought my brother out I had the

opportunity to hire the husband of one of my wife's good friends," says Bill. "Arnold Dreyer had been the Regional Director of IRS for about six states. I think he'd always wondered if he could make it in the private sector. He was 59 and wanted to work another six years. He was really a genius at business administration."

A short, quiet man whose highest priority was looking after both the company and Bill Dunn, Dreyer brought J.E. Dunn Construction up-to-date administratively. Always pleasant but reserved, he could confront difficult issues.

The Aldersgate Village apartments in Topeka in 1978 represented one of J.E. Dunn's first joint ventures, but even more interesting than the joint venture aspect is the way the job was won.

Mike Barr remembers a woman from the Aldersgate Church asking Bill Dunn Sr., "Do you intend to build our facility in a Christian-like manner?"

"Bill explained to her that the construction company would do the job for a guaranteed maximum price with any savings being returned to the church" says Mike. "He stressed that J.E. Dunn lives and dies by bringing projects to their clients on time. Mr. Dunn also said he would nail down the suppliers and get good qualified bids from subcontractors. He kept hitting home the fact that we would be fair, reasonable, and hard-working. By the time he was done, the lady was won over. There wasn't any doubt we would be doing this job."

On the drive home, Mike commented to Mr. Dunn on the effect his words had on everyone. "Tell me where I'm exaggerating," Bill said.

"With Mr. Dunn, it's from the heart."

Dale Shikles helped J.E. Dunn revamp its accounting systems in the 1970s.

Dreyer moved first to update the antiquated filing systems. He had Ardyth and Billie hire a file clerk and then established guidelines to determine how long accounting records were kept. They moved the files to Dunleith Towers' basement, where they were logged and sent to the warehouse. A few files remain missing, according to Billie, "because some of the ledgers were just on shelves against the wall and had been eaten by termites."

Because the warehouse was susceptible to fire and only had limited space, all the files were eventually moved out to the caves, a natural underground rock formation southeast of town in which space had been converted for business use.

In early 1974 Arnold Dreyer hired Dale Shikles, an accountant from Arthur Andersen, and charged him with revamping the accounting systems.

"Because of his Internal Revenue Service background," says Dale, "[Arnold] had some titles that were very synonymous with those used by the IRS. So, his first title for me was 'Chief Accountant,' I think. It was an interesting time. The big changeover was in process."

Dale faced a mountain of paperwork. "I think there were somewhere between 300 and 400 people on a manual payroll. Everything was manual. For a manual payroll system, it was actually very efficient for meeting deadlines, but the rest of the accounting system was very poor and couldn't generate reports on a timely basis. Everyone wanted to go to computers, but first we had to get the manual system working well, which took about two years."

Dale in turn enlisted Sandy Comley, now in charge of the payroll department with a weekly payroll of 1,750. He also hired Barbara Rathbun to help get the manual system under control. Barbara would eventually take the lead in overseeing the conversion to computers.

In addition to changing basic procedures and slowly upgrading the technology, Arnold and Dale engineered a switch from "completed contract accounting" to the

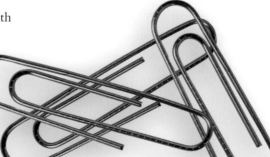

"percentage of completion" method. While standard today, "percentage of completion" accounting was not commonplace in 1974. "Percentage of completion" allows management a much clearer picture of its business because it analyzes revenue against the percentage of a project that is actually complete at that moment, thereby allowing for accurate audits. "Completed contract accounting," on the other hand, defers all revenues from a project until it is complete, which can lead to problematic peaks and valleys in the numbers. Eventually, Dale placed J.E. Dunn's accounting business with the firm of Grant Thornton, who would remain the company's auditor for many years.

Finally, Arnold created a personnel department. "We were growing," says Bill Dunn, "and all of a sudden we had 65 people in the office instead of 35 and we didn't have a human resources department, which in those days was called a personnel department. And so Arnold Dreyer told Ardyth Wendte, 'I know it's not a job you want, but we need someone to run the personnel department.'"

"Arnold did a very fine job of managing and he taught me a lot," reports Wendte, "He enjoyed his role at J.E. Dunn and often referred to himself as 'the point of the lance.'"

Ardyth Wendte remembers the years of administrative restructuring as both challenging and rewarding. "When the company was small and you had been there from the beginning to see so much growth and change, you did a lot of different things because there wasn't the tremendous volume for each activity. So, you wore many hats. You did whatever was required. I learned a lot about personnel matters, such as hiring and benefits, purchasing office equipment and furnishings, government laws and regulations, and day-to-day problem solving. No two days were ever the same."

"No one did more than Bill Dunn," she points out. "[He] worked night and day and put everything he had into the company. He laid the groundwork that the company is built on now and instilled optimism and confidence in those around him. He was involved in every phase from marketing to bidding to project completion."

From the larger perspective, J.E. Dunn Construction was trying to bring its homespun management systems in line with its big-time construction abilities. "Arnold, Bernard Jacquinot, and myself were the three directors of the company," says Bill. "We had some excellent people in construction, estimating, and in project management, but we had a weakness in business administration. Arnold Dreyer solved that problem for us. He was a huge asset as far as righting the ship. He was the one who brought rhyme and reason to our business administration."

Equipment, both purchased and rented, represents a costly line item for any general contractor. To the great benefit of the company's bottom line, Bill Dunn Jr. made the economics of equipment his special area of interest.

"In 1979, I went back to school to get an MBA at Rockhurst College, where my thesis was on designing equipment purchasing systems for the construction industry. For the thesis, I traced key equipment costs with Jess Hunt and Bernard Jacquinot at the J.E. Dunn warehouse. We created a historical database to support the systems."

The company adopted Bill Jr.'s system for buying, selling, and leasing equipment in 1980. If the rate of return was over 20 percent, the purchase would be considered. In terms of equipment rental, and in order to make certain that owners wouldn't be overcharged and everyone would save money during the process, the company would charge less than market rates.

Bill Dunn Jr. (above) refined J.E. Dunn's approach to buying, selling, and leasing equipment such as the tower crane (below).

(left) Building No. 40, one of the more impressive structures that J.E. Dunn built at Corporate Woods.

(above) San Francisco Towers Condominiums and Santa Fe Apartments at Crown Center in Kansas City.

Other Critical Hires

*B*ill Dunn's interest was in construction, not real estate, but the real estate side of the business had to be managed until it was sold. For this purpose, Bill hired his son Steve in March 1975. Recently out of Rockhurst College, Steve was the son with the "street smarts," according to his father. He was immediately assigned to work under Arnold Dreyer.

Of his early years with the company, Steve says: "I learned a lot from Arnold. He taught me a lot about analyzing a situation before you make a decision. I'll always be grateful for my experience with Arnold."

At the same time, Bill also hired his oldest son, Bill Jr., who had worked in sales for his uncles at Aylward Products, a building materials and equipment company.

"I worked under Bernard Jacquinot, who was training me to be a project manager," says Bill Jr. "They didn't give me much to do at first and I got bored. After a few months I asked to get involved in purchasing. I'm an accomplishment-driven person and thought I could contribute early on in purchasing with my background in selling construction materials and equipment at Aylward Products. The company had a negative net worth at the time and I wanted to do something right away that would be profitable for it. I knew how to get good prices and I knew how to talk to salesmen."

Barry Brady, a young executive with Business Men's Assurance Company, also came to J.E. Dunn as part of the new administrative reshuffling in 1975. After working for J.E. Dunn in finance, real estate, safety, and affirmative action for a few years, he was named senior vice president of administration, overseeing all areas of human resources and finance.

Three Major New Projects

*S*hortly after purchasing J.E. Dunn from his brother, Bill Sr. had three new high profile construction projects in his crosshairs. The Truman Medical Center, the San Francisco Towers Condominiums and Santa Fe Apartments, and Corporate Woods would all prove to be important to the survival of the company, and as a group would bear a large share of the burden of bringing J.E. Dunn out of debt.

Truman Medical Center was a pivotal job for J.E. Dunn in the 1970s.

Steve Dunn, Chairman of J.E. Dunn Construction Company, articulates a central tenet of the J.E. Dunn business philosophy, one that began with Ernie Dunn in the first half of the 20th century.

"You have to think about the long-term, providing quality work for your clients, and putting the client first. If you're in it just to see how much money you can make on a particular job regardless of whether the customer is happy, you won't be in this business for long. Reputation is everything in this business."

The overriding truth of the statement is evident in the fact that over 80 percent of J.E. Dunn's business comes through repeat business or referrals. It simply would not occur without satisfied customers.

Metropolitan Life Insurance Company is an excellent example. "Met Life was the thunder behind Corporate Woods," explains Bill Dunn Sr. "They liked what we were doing and asked us to build a small office campus in Tulsa. We built several buildings, parking garages, and hotels down there."

Trust generates repeat and referral business. "Owners trust us," points out General Superintendent Tom Turner. "With DST we are on the third or fourth job. We were able to negotiate their Cathedral Square project in downtown Kansas City in a matter of 30 minutes. They trust us that much."

DST Systems Inc. is one of many customers to reward J.E. Dunn with repeat business. The above photographs show interior and exterior scenes at DST's Winchester Data Center, built by J.E. Dunn.

The Truman Medical Center was the first of the three to break ground, in June of 1974, barely four months after J.E. Dunn's management had changed. Connected to the north end of the UMKC Medical School Building, the medical center was designed as a 326-bed hospital to replace the 70-year-old General Hospital Building at 24th and Cherry. Won in a lump-sum bid of nearly $24 million, Truman Medical Center would be J.E. Dunn's highest profile project since completing Worlds of Fun.

At the time, says Bill Sr., "we were holding our breath as to whether or not we were going to survive...That was a very important project to the survival of this company and it was a very important project pointing out the need for us to be on the cutting edge of new methods, new materials, and new equipment."

The new equipment and methods were proposed when Bill Sr. convinced the superintendent, Jack McCollom, to buy and use two climbing cranes. "I really almost had to pull rank to get Jack to even be interested in using those," he says, "because we'd only used them once before. This was down on the Vista Del Rio project, which was a 19-story building."

Jack, who passed away in 1989, was one of the savviest of all superintendents in terms of doing more with less, but was very leery of spending money on new technology.

"We made quite a believer out of him when the cranes saved a million dollars in labor at Truman," Bill Sr. says. "Where normally we would have built hoist towers outside the building and needed workers to carry steel and the forms throughout the 500-foot long structure, the cranes could pick up these materials outside and place them wherever they needed to go inside the building."

The cranes used at Truman Medical Center in 1975 were more complicated than today's versions. In contrast to modern cranes that are set up outside a building, the old climbing cranes were jacked up floor by floor through the center of the building. The various openings where the crane had been located had to be closed at the end of the job.

The Truman Medical Center topped out in 1975 and was finished in 1976. The cranes were cheaper than today's half-million dollar models, but they represented one of the most radical changes in construction at the time.

A month later, J.E. Dunn landed one of the biggest projects it would have for another quarter century. Corporate Woods, a proposed office park in Johnson County, Kan., provided projects for the next twenty years, and more importantly, helped set the tone for many of the construction management and design/build philosophies that still guide the company in the 21st century.

Set on a 294-acre site at College Boulevard and Indian Creek Parkway in Overland Park, Corporate Woods was financed by Metropolitan Life Insurance Company. Access to the area was made possible because of the new I-435 highway looping around the city. Overland Park would soon become an urban center with the help of Corporate Woods. The development was designed to blend in with the natural surroundings.

Conceived as 29 buildings with an expected price tag of $250 million, the office park was an early example of a negotiated bid, an important element in J.E. Dunn's preconstruction services. In negotiated bid projects, the general contractor negotiates the price at the beginning with the owner.

The negotiated bid process sprang in part from the troubled economy and rising costs of the early 1970s. In Kansas City, the strikes of 1969 and 1970 had doubled wages. Budgets became more and more difficult to meet, and in that climate, owners and architects were struggling to meet their fiscal goals.

Building No.32 at Corporate Woods.

"Owners and architects were having a terrible time trying to figure out what their budget should be," says Bill Sr. "Prior to that time they rarely even talked to us. They looked on general contractors as villains that you build a cage around. Then they started coming to us. I'd been doing this for years for several other clients, where they would say 'we have 'x' number of dollars to spend on this project, here's the square footage, tell us what type of materials and how you'd go about it.'"

"We had worked very closely with some owners and architects even before

Chuck Cianciaruso, head of marketing at J.E. Dunn, joined the company during the construction of Corporate Woods.

the strikes, but after the strikes is when the negotiated work really started to come to fruition," says Terry Dunn. Tom Congleton, Chairman of Jones and Company Realtors, who developed Corporate Woods, was among the first owners to negotiate a bid with the contractor of his choice. He would then depend on that contractor for preconstruction services. J.E. Dunn was of course happy with a design/build approach that allowed them to 'value engineer' the entire project, and to seek solutions that would keep costs as low as possible for the owner. After Corporate Woods was built, Tom Congleton negotiated and sought preconstruction services on every contract for Jones and Company.

In addition to their preconstruction services, J.E. Dunn's progressive concept of 'guaranteed maximum savings' – returning savings on a job to an owner as they had done with Worlds of Fun – secured Jones and Company's business for many projects over the next two decades. This established an important business model for J.E. Dunn; repeat and referral business became the backbone of J.E. Dunn's client list, running in excess of 75 percent of overall business in the nearly 30 years since the buyout.

Corporate Woods proved to be something of an incubator for J.E. Dunn. Charlie Wakeman was the original superintendent, and new hires, such as future superintendent Rick Fortner, cut their teeth on the project. In addition, Chuck Cianciaruso, J.E. Dunn's longtime marketing chief, also came to the company through Corporate Woods. An executive vice president of a large architectural engineering company working on the office park, he was dissatisfied with his arrangement, and jumped when Bill Sr. offered him a position as head of marketing at J.E. Dunn.

In October of 1974, three months after it had broken ground at Corporate Woods, J.E. Dunn began its third major project of the year: the 249-unit Santa Fe Apartments and the 28-story San Francisco

Condominium Tower, both Crown Center developments.

Because J.E. Dunn had established a design/build relationship with Crown Center, its stores, restaurants, and entertainment complexes added over the next ten years would all be awarded to J.E. Dunn as well.

The Crown Center project, like Corporate Woods, was a negotiated bid, partially because of its success with earlier clients, and partially because of inflation. "Prices started escalating, and in the late 1970s, interest rates were running close to 20 percent," notes Terry Dunn. "There was a tremendous need for owners to lock in prices and to have jobs completed by the earliest possible date. To do that they began negotiating with contractors who could deliver the work on time and within their budgets."

Partnering with Labor

*B*y the mid-1970s, work was steady enough that J.E. Dunn could offer new benefits to some of its field employees. Typically, superintendents and foremen had been laid off when a job was completed, which saved contractors the expense of keeping people when times were slow. J.E. Dunn changed the relationship, putting its field supervisory personnel

J.E. Dunn has continued to build for Crown Center for nearly 30 years. The construction company completed the 2600 Grand Crown Center building in 1991.

During the Kansas City labor strikes of 1969 and 1970, it seemed as if labor and management were fated to be adversaries to the bitter end. A major thaw in the relationship wouldn't come until 1979 with the establishment of the Labor Management Council of Greater Kansas City, an organization that was created as an afterthought.

"In 1979, the federal government threatened to shut down industrial construction projects in Missouri if the state legislature didn't pass laws that complied with the Environmental Protection Agency's standards on air quality," Bill Dunn Sr. explains. "The Missouri legislature's failure to enact the laws would have hurt both the unions and businesses."

The shutdown was imminent that spring when the Missouri Senate looked like it was going to

Bill Dunn Sr.

let two bills on the matter die. As immediate past president of the Chamber of Commerce of Greater Kansas City and chairman of its labor-management committee, Bill approached Meyer Goldman, editor of *The Labor Beacon*, and asked his help in putting together a statewide coalition of labor and business leaders. "When the coalition met with legislators in Jefferson City, the lawmakers were in shock. They'd never seen labor and management ask for anything jointly. And we were amazed at how quickly they passed the laws," Bill recalls.

After the coalition's success in Jefferson City, local business and labor leaders decided to form a permanent organization, the Labor Management Council of Greater Kansas City, which would be chaired jointly by business and labor representatives. Bill was named its first business chairman. "We worked on issues that were affecting life and safety and issues of importance to the overall community. We found that labor

and management probably agreed on about 90 percent of the issues."

When Bill retired from the council several years ago, Tom Whittaker, one of J.E. Dunn's in-house attorneys, stepped in as a representative for the construction company. "Well over a hundred actions have been taken by council – actions that are beneficial to society," Bill says.

Tom Whittaker.

The effort with the LMC and a positive working relationship with the unions has paid off for J.E. Dunn. "We would not have succeeded at the Woodlands Racetrack without our good relationship with labor," says Bill. "And when the W.W. Grainger people came from Chicago and asked labor what construction company they would recommend to build a million square foot warehouse, labor recommended J.E. Dunn."

Tom Turner, a general superintendent for J.E. Dunn.

on 'straight time,' guaranteeing them an income and benefits independent of any particular project.

Radical as it seemed, putting field supervisory forces on straight time and providing benefits was consistent with the philosophy of establishing sound and loyal relationships, whether with clients or employees. Looking to the long-term on the employee side of the equation, Bill Sr. felt that 1) it was "the right thing to do," a principle that guided most of his business decisions, and 2) the long-term savings from loyalty would outstrip the short-term savings from laying people off and hiring them back later.

Tom Turner, a general superintendent who joined the company in 1979, speaks to the policy. "You're more than a used and abused body out there. J.E. Dunn gives you a career. Not all construction companies

do that. For example, we have a cement finisher foreman who used to get laid off when the job was over before he joined J.E. Dunn. Now that he's with Dunn he's bought a house and bass boat and was able to take a *paid* vacation for the first time ever with his wife and kids."

Terry Dunn, now president and CEO of J.E. Dunn Construction, explains the pragmatism behind the philosophy, and its extension to clients as well as employees. "For us, enlightened self-interest means treating clients, architects, engineers, and the public-at-large as you would want to be treated yourself. This philosophy is one of the main reasons our company will last."

J.E. Dunn's visibility through major projects such as the Truman Medical Center and Corporate Woods led to further civic involvement for Bill Sr., and by 1977 he was president of the Kansas City Chamber of Commerce. His work at the Chamber, combined with his good relationship and track record with labor, led to one of the most significant examples of creative leadership in the company's history. When the need arose to get labor and management to find mutual solutions to critical issues in construction, and also to get critical legislation passed in Missouri, J.E. Dunn helped create the Labor Management Council. The council brought leaders from both sides of the

table together to address thorny issues such as insurance, safety, and legislation.

Skip Hutton, former president of the Builders' Association of Missouri notes that the work with the Labor Management Council began a long relationship between J.E. Dunn Construction and labor. "Bernard Jacquinot and Bill Dunn's sons have been very active in labor relations. These representatives have been key to getting good contracts. Bill Sr. was very involved with this. They try to avoid confrontation, and try to understand both sides. They have been very good at getting their peers in the industry to go along with the agreements that have been worked out."

Establishing a Foothold in Health Care

*T*wo other major projects that stood out after the buyout were St. Joseph Medical Center, begun in March of 1975, and Shawnee Mission Medical Center, begun in June of 1975.

The $23 million St. Joseph project included a medical office building, an elevated parking garage, and a 300-bed acute care hospital at I-435 and State Line Road. The Sisters of St. Joseph of Carondelet would run the new hospital serving the growing populations of

J.E. Dunn workers dug out this tunnel during an addition to St. Joseph Health Center.

An addition at St. Joseph Health Center was very problematic because of the need to build a tunnel between the addition and the hospital proper as quietly as possible.

The tunnel had to be dug under an existing building which housed the emergency room and its attending operating rooms. Because of the nature of the business overhead, no noise could be tolerated in the construction – no generators, drills, or any other kind of loud machine.

The solution: three men with pneumatic chipping hammers and a rotary grinding head hand dug a 14 feet high by 120 feet long tunnel, four feet under the floor of the operating rooms. Debris was moved after every two feet of progress and fresh air was circulated at all times. Twelve weeks after they began, they sawed through a 12-inch foundation wall of the existing building. "They never knew we were underneath them," says Steve Hoye, project superintendent.

southern Jackson County and southern Johnson County, people who did not have medical facilities nearby.

Shawnee Mission Medical Center was an $18 million expansion and renovation of an existing facility. J.E. Dunn added service areas for emergency, ambulatory, therapeutic, and diagnostic care and increased the number of hospital beds by 265. Bob Dunn, Bill's fifth son, got his first taste of the construction business while working as a laborer at this site.

Solidifying their reputation as the premier general contractor for health care facilities in the area, J.E. Dunn also had hospital construction underway in Smithville, Raytown, Overland Park, south Kansas City, and Olathe.

Jim Griffin, a J.E. Dunn general superintendent specializing in hospitals, notes that the construction company brings doctors, nurses, and other hospital personnel into the planning process by providing them with a mock-up for approval before the work begins. Jim R. Miller, who heads up J.E. Dunn's health care division, discusses some of the unique aspects of the work: "We spend a tremendous amount of time on preconstruction services in health care. It can take months, even years, to work out estimating, scheduling, and logistics issues, especially on hospital expansions where

it's important to build without interfering with day-to-day operations."

Projects outside of health, such as a 200,000 square foot distribution center for Sony at the Airworld Complex near the Kansas City International Airport, and a 975,000 square foot addition for Sears Distribution Center, kept J.E. Dunn busy. The $50 million Sears work, begun in 1977, gave Terry Dunn his first experience as a project manager on a large-scale job. Both jobs added to J.E. Dunn's expanding relationships with national and international corporations.

Agents of Change

*B*y 1977, Bill Sr., Steve Dunn, and Barry Brady decided to focus on construction, and began to sell the real estate holdings. With Truman Medical Center, Corporate Woods, Crown Center, and other projects completed, and with more work in the pipeline, Bill Dunn was able to pay off his brother in late 1977, two years early.

The increasing volume of work required some changes in how projects were managed. Organization, planning, estimating, and scheduling grew in importance as the company was juggling 30 or more jobs at any one time. Bill Sr. kept his eye out for people who had the skills to handle the workload.

J.E. Dunn worked at Shawnee Mission Medical Center in the 1970s and returned in the 1990s to build the colorful children's wing (pictured).

Like Arnold Dreyer, Lou Hilker proved to be the right man at the right time. Hilker had come to Bill Sr.'s attention through his involvement with both the Penn Valley Community College and the Worlds of Fun projects.

"With the poor weather conditions, we couldn't have done [the Worlds of Fun] project in one year without his help," remembers Bill Sr. "Finally, Lou came in one day, and he said 'I'm not real happy with my present job.' I told him that I'd like J.E. Dunn to be the first contractor in Kansas City with its own in-house critical path scheduler. Lou has been an asset to the company ever since."

Hilker found his position quite fluid. "At J.E. Dunn, I did the scheduling at first, and then my role shifted to quality control and running progress meetings for different projects. I work as a proponent of change in the company, almost in a consultant role. I've forced a lot of change on the TQM (Total Quality Management)."

By way of example, in the early 1990s, Hilker was one of the authors of the *Associated General Contractors Total Quality Management Book for Construction*, organized and edited by a professor at Iowa State. The book, which addresses ways to improve the business of construction, has become something of a bible in the industry.

As the company grew, Hilker was often in charge of managing the growth, and therefore helped pioneer some early joint venture projects, such as a hospital in Moberly, Mo., with a contractor named B.D. Simon out of Columbia, and a hospital, retirement community, and shoe warehouse with Lee & Beutel in Topeka, Kan.

Hilker's talents for finding cutting edge systems and processes allowed J.E. Dunn

Penn Valley Community College, where Lou Hilker's skills in critical path scheduling helped J.E. Dunn meet a tight construction deadline.

to expand its range because it could work efficiently, keep to schedules, and share technologies and systems among jobs. With many people on straight time, this became important.

But Lou Hilker was not the only agent of change at J.E. Dunn in the late

1970s. Bernard Jacquinot shifted his focus to operational matters and handling the warehouse and all field operations including labor negotiations.

Also working in operations, Bill Dunn Jr. applied his energies to equipment management. For example, he points out that "a lot of contractors don't keep track of lumber and small tools. If they buy small equipment for a particular job they don't give themselves a credit for it – they just move this stuff from job to job and it's never accounted for. What we do is give credit for materials that are left over at the end of a job." This seems a small thing, but with many jobs, the numbers add up.

Bill Jr. went on to earn a masters degree in business administration at Rockhurst College where he developed a system for equipment management and purchasing that the company has used ever since.

New Growth

By the end of the 1970s, J.E. Dunn was tackling projects as diverse as the Avila College Library and Education Center, the Kansas City Apparel Mart, and Aldersgate Village in Topeka. In subsequent years, high-tech centers, prisons, and schools would add to this portfolio.

By the end of the decade, J.E. Dunn had every reason to be proud. They had survived the buyout, the years of negative net worth, the Kemper Arena collapse, and the recession of the mid-1970s, and had reassumed control of the company from its creditors. They had built on a half-century of business by erecting well-known structures in Kansas City, such as Worlds of Fun; Corporate Woods; hospitals such as St. Joseph, Truman, and Shawnee Mission; local landmarks such as Santa Fe Condominiums and San Francisco Towers Apartments, and Kemper Arena; and distribution centers for major companies such as Sears, W.W. Grainger, and Sony.

For 1979, J.E. Dunn Construction had revenues of $69.1 million. *Engineering News-Record* ranked it the 250th largest contractor in the United States based on its new contracts for the year. With a positive net worth and entirely revamped office systems and procedures, J.E. Dunn was prepared for growth in the 1980s and 1990s.

Chapter 5
NEW HORIZONS
1980-1991

J.E. Dunn's tenant finish work at the Shook, Hardy
& Bacon law offices involved extensive millwork.

EARLY 1980s RECESSION

Downturn

THE 1980s BROUGHT WITH IT NOT ONLY AN UPCOMING PRESIDENTIAL ELECTION BETWEEN INCUMBENT JIMMY CARTER AND CALIFORNIA GOVERNOR RONALD REAGAN, BUT ANOTHER RECESSION, WHICH LASTED NEARLY THREE YEARS. IN JUNE 1980, MANY THOUGHT THE RECESSION WAS ENDING AFTER JUST A FEW MONTHS, BUT BUSINESS TURNED SOUR AGAIN IN MID-1981 AND REMAINED SO UNTIL LATE 1982.

Like everything else, construction slowed a bit during this period, but J.E. Dunn's long-term contracts carried it through. In particular, Corporate Woods, with four buildings underway in 1980, remained a major focus. Many other schools, offices, and hospitals filled out the project list.

One project, however, brought a challenge that is representative of the many pitfalls in the industry. Jackson County had $25 million available for a detention and courts facility, as well as a 230,000 square foot two-building complex consisting of a 13-story, 560-cell prison and a four-story court building. The chairman of the county legislature had pledged to keep the cost to $24.5 million. J.E. Dunn won the contract with a bid of $28.15 million, but an attorney

who claimed he represented "concerned taxpayers" requested new bids be made on the project based on the fact that the winning bid was over $3 million higher than the approved figure. Further, his challenge stated that "any award to Dunn based on any variance from the bid documents or for any sum less than the bid by Dunn would violate state laws."

Many suspected the attorney really represented another contractor seeking a second chance to bid. In the face of the

challenge, the county had three choices: seek a new bid, redesign the buildings, or proceed at the higher rate. Delays would cost $10,000 per day. In the end, the challenge was rebuffed, and the county continued with J.E. Dunn, who value-engineered the project for $26.58 million, nearly $1.5 million under their original bid. The project represented a foothold in what would become a specialty for J.E. Dunn: correctional facilities.

(left) The Jackson County Detention Center represented one of J.E. Dunn's early forays in correctional facility construction.

(far left) J.E. Dunn workers build the Jackson County Detention Center in downtown Kansas City. Behind them towers the Southwestern Bell Telephone Building, where J.E. Dunn crews had worked a decade earlier.

Core Values

One new administrative development, the founding of the Dunn Family Foundation, served to institutionalize core values in the early 1980s. Prior to 1981, philanthropy had represented a central pillar of both the family and the company. Ernie Dunn Sr. had gained fame for refusing a profit on the Quartermaster Depot Project during World War II, and was known in Catholic circles for performing services for the Benedictine Convent and other Catholic institutions at no fee. Less well-known were his acts of generosity to both individuals and institutions, such as the Humboldt School one block south of the office, for which he quietly bought clothing and school supplies for the students.

Bill Sr.'s many personal civic involvements, along with those of the third generation, were also matched by corporate and personal philanthropy. In the early 1980s, with the company growing, attorney Larry Bingham advised

the Dunns that a more formal structure might increase the effectiveness of their giving while providing more organization and consistency.

Tax strategies were also a consideration in forming the Dunn Family Foundation. According to Bingham, Bill Dunn "never pushed the envelope as far as taxes go – he was very conservative and very fair." But there was nothing radical or unfair about initiating a foundation, which could utilize tax advantages to the benefit of those to whom the Dunns wished to make contributions.

"I was involved with the forming of the Dunn Family Foundation," says Ardyth Wendte. "The Clearinghouse for Mid-Continent Foundations provided us with specifics for establishing a foundation, and the legalities were handled by Larry Bingham."

"Although we started out pretty small, eventually more and more giving was channeled through the Foundation." Ardyth explains that, "Requests came to me, which I would then submit to the Foundation board at their quarterly meetings. Occasionally Steve Dunn and I would make an on-site visit to some of the charitable locations and report our findings at the meetings. Eventually, as my other corporate duties increased, Billie Hestand took this over. The Foundation's emphasis then was the same as it is today – education, health, and human services, youth, the disabled, the elderly, ethnic minorities, and community development in the Kansas City area." The Foundation also makes some contributions outside the Kansas City area.

Another example of community involvement that began in the early 1980s is recounted by Jack Steadman of Hunt Enterprises. "It was about 1982 when the Chiefs organization decided to do something to benefit children's charities. At the same time, Bill Dunn was trying to get funds to match a Mabee Foundation grant for an inner city children's program (the Niles Home for Children). He invited me to a breakfast where he asked members of the business community if they would help meet this grant. It struck me that our benefit game could be tied to that project, which it then was. The game raised the funds necessary to match the Mabee Foundation Challenge grant."

"Since that time, the Dunn family has been involved in the benefit game with us – not just Bill Dunn Sr., but Bill Jr., and Bob – to the point that we call it the 'Dunn Deal.' I think we are now approaching $4.5 million raised over the years for children's benefits, and I give the

Liz Nace, secretary of the Dunn Family Foundation and administrative assistant at J.E. Dunn, and Bob Dunn deal with hundreds of charitable requests yearly for the family foundation.

Dunns much of the credit. They make the contacts and they get the money in from contractors, subcontractors, and suppliers. The last several years we've tied it to a joint project for the Boys and Girls Clubs and the Don Bosco Center. Benefits from the game had climbed to about $356,000 per year by the year 2002."

"Bill Dunn is the silent guardian for poor children in Kansas City," says Randall O'Donnell, president and CEO of the Children's Mercy Hospitals and Clinics. "He has fostered a very unique culture at J.E. Dunn of giving and meeting community needs."

General Superintendent Jack McCollom (left) came out of retirement to manage the rebuilding of the Hyatt Regency Hotel lobby after the skywalks collapsed.

The Life and Death Nature of Construction and the Need for Quality Assurance

*T*he most notable event in the field during this period was another tragedy, just over two years after the Kemper cave-in. This one was much worse, costing over 100 lives, but it involved a building with which J.E. Dunn had no previous connection.

On July 17, 1981, guests at the brand new Hyatt Regency Hotel in Kansas City were gathered for a tea dance in the hotel's lobby. While the majority were on the ground level, some were dancing on the skywalks on the second, third, and fourth levels. At about 7:05 p.m., amid the dancing and the music and the tinkling of glasses, many people heard a loud crack and looked up. Others heard nothing, but the second and fourth level walkways were giving way overhead. Concrete, iron, and masonry crashed upon the ground floor, trapping victims in the debris.

The next day, Jack McCollom, a retired general superintendent, called Bill Sr. "They're going to need help on this," he said. "I'd like to come out of retirement and do this project because it's going to be a mess." McCollom had been in damage control on a battleship in World War II and was experienced in situations in which people had been killed or injured.

J.E. Dunn offered its services at cost and set immediately to work. Under McCollom's leadership, the company had the lobby back in shape in three to four months, replacing all skywalks with a mezzanine to connect the north and south parts of the building.

By 1982, the business climate was still a problem. Nearly 25,000 jobs had been lost from the local economy in 33 months, and 60,000 people were on unemployment. At J.E. Dunn, revenue was down about 10 percent, but the company had embarked on another downtown project: the Vista International Hotel.

Even before the hotel was finished, the newspapers referred to the Vista as a miracle, largely because of its nine-year history of complex financing that ultimately involved 32 banks, insurance companies, businesses, and charitable organizations.

Once the hotel had been financed, however, general contractor J.E. Dunn ran into problems. "They had a West Coast designer and we were concerned about his knowledge of construction in the Midwest. So we had a structural engineer look at the building, and they were concerned about a number of issues," says Bill Sr.

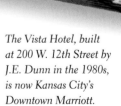

The Vista Hotel, built at 200 W. 12th Street by J.E. Dunn in the 1980s, is now Kansas City's Downtown Marriott.

"We built a mock-up of the outside wall in a laboratory of the Heitman Company, a St. Louis firm that we still use today for checking building exteriors. The mock-up showed that if we built it the way it was specified it would leak like a sieve. I would probably have been hung at 10th and Main if we'd done that. These problems were corrected in cooperation with the design team."

Bill Sr. had been in favor of peer review since the similarly named Vista del Rio project in the late 1960s. A consulting structural engineer found that without revising the structural plan the Vista del Rio would have fallen as soon as it was constructed.

Since the construction of the Vista del Rio, Bill Sr. had emphasized the importance of quality assurance – not only doing a quality job as designed, but to double check the plans before building. "People ask how we can afford that," says Bill Sr. "I say to them 'I don't know how we can't afford it.' Quality assurance is the same as an insurance policy."

Testing the Waters for Expansion

Yet another proposed hotel, this one in Tulsa, helped usher in an important new idea for J.E. Dunn, and ultimately, ten years later, an entirely new era. Metropolitan Life Insurance Company, the funding entity behind Corporate Woods, wanted to build an office park in Tulsa, including several office buildings, garages, and a hotel, and sought the assistance of their Corporate Woods contractor, J.E. Dunn.

The Warren Place Doubletree Hotel in Tulsa would be a $19 million, 371-room, 10-floor luxury hotel. It was notable for two reasons. Borrowing on the success of the Vista process, J.E. Dunn again used mock-ups to assure the hotel rooms would be sound. More importantly, however, the Warren Place project set in motion the idea of J.E. Dunn being a regional, as opposed to merely a local, contractor.

Senior vice president Mike Barr, then a project manager who had been working in the office under senior project manager Fred Shipman, was asked to head up the Tulsa office, becoming the first J.E. Dunn employee to move to a post outside of Kansas City. "I had the opportunity to

The Warren Place Doubletree Hotel in Tulsa.

try a lot of leading edge things," Mike says. "I was also the first one to do a joint venture," referring to the Aldersgate project in Topeka in 1978. The message seemed to be if you think you're big enough to go do this project, then just go do it!"

If J.E. Dunn was going to expand, it needed to be aggressive and look for a second market beyond Tulsa. Terry Dunn, executive vice president in project management at the time, put it this way: "We wanted to grow. If you sit for a day, you take a step back."

St. Louis was struggling with a challenging labor situation at the time, but Denver was booming. J.E. Dunn had some clients with interests in Denver, so the decision was made to open there as well. An executive from a Denver firm was hired to run the office. The company had no other foothold in the Mile High City, so, according to Chuck Cianciaruso, "we pounded the pavement to make contacts. Opening the Denver office proved to be the challenge that tested the company's commitment to regional growth."

The administrative structure to handle expansion had been established a year or two before with the creation of Dunn Industries, a holding company for J.E. Dunn's various business interests, including construction, real estate, equity

management, the Dunn Family Foundation, and any future expansion, including the Tulsa and Denver offices. The original J.E. Dunn Construction Company of Kansas City was now just another subsidiary of Dunn Industries.

After building the Doubletree Hotel and other office buildings and garages in Tulsa, Metropolitan Life Insurance decided somewhat suddenly to get out of real estate investments. In spite of the Met Life decision, and given its commitment to expansion, J.E. Dunn decided to stay in the Tulsa market. Unfortunately, Mike Barr was certain he was not in Kansas anymore when he made the low bid on the Tulsa airport and still lost the contract. It was the first of numerous such occurrences.

"We learned a hard lesson," says Bill Sr. "[Mike] would bid a job and he'd be low bidder and they'd find some way to throw out all the bids and then maybe end up negotiating with one of the hometown people. When you're the new kid on the block you get 'hometowned.' " The Denver office was struggling as well.

J.E. Dunn didn't win every job at home during this period either. At about the same time as it was opening the Tulsa office, the company submitted the low bid to the Kansas City, Mo., City Council on the Auditorium Plaza Garage and the

Barney Allis Plaza Park, which was to be on top of the garage. After the bids were in, the city eliminated some of the original items, and then awarded the project to another contractor. Angry at being squeezed out, Barry Brady spoke for the rest of the J.E. Dunn executives. "It seems as though the City Council changed their minds," he said simply to the media.[23]

New Companies, New Insurance, and Changes at the Top

By 1985, J.E. Dunn had $185 million in revenues, making it the 108th largest general contractor in the country. The company had field personnel that ranged from 250 to 600, depending on the amount of work underway, and 90 people working in the office on Holmes Street. In five years, half of which had been in a recession, J.E. Dunn had grown 288 percent in terms of annual revenue.

Despite all the recent upgrades, the company's growth continued to require administrative change. With office staff

The PPG Biomedical Systems building was one of more than 20 projects that J.E. Dunn built in the Southlake Technology Park in Lenexa, Kan., beginning in the late 1980s. Hugh Zimmer, president of the Zimmer Companies, was the owner and developer at Southlake, and has worked with J.E. Dunn on several projects since.

Elmer Bishop, former J.E. Dunn general superintendent, oversaw construction of the tower at the AT&T Town Pavilion.

increasing in numbers, Dave Foster, a young executive from Waddell & Reed, was hired to assist Ardyth Wendte with hiring, training, and benefits administration. He proved to be invaluable in human resources, and took over when Ardyth retired in 1993.

On the organizational side, Dunn Realty was formed to manage new real estate interests, which included some joint projects and holdings with construction clients, as well as the company's own properties such as the J.E. Dunn offices, warehouses, and apartment complexes in Warrensburg, Mo. These apartments had been returned to J.E. Dunn when

the purchaser was unable to make the mortgage payments.

J.E. Dunn was also questioning the level of service it was receiving from its existing insurance brokers, particularly its umbrella coverage. With a new agent, David Lockton of Lockton Insurance, a group of J.E. Dunn executives from project management, quality control, safety, and legal, met with decision-makers from several insurance and bonding companies.

"Each J.E. Dunn executive talked about his way of doing business," reports Lockton. "The highlight was Bill Dunn Sr. coming into the room to discuss why J.E. Dunn set up the quality assurance program. It wasn't directly related to insurance, but yet it was, because one of the major sources of insurance claims is what we call 'completed operations.' Every single insurance company representative left those meetings knowing that this was an extremely unique contractor and that there was less exposure with them than any other contractor they had come into contact with."

After the meetings J.E. Dunn's casualty insurance policy was renewed with significantly lower premiums based on its record and its approach to doing business.

Perhaps the most important administrative changes involved major promotions for three members of the third generation. In 1985, Terry was

named executive vice president in charge of construction operations; Steve, vice president of administration and financing; and Bill Jr., vice president of purchasing, warehousing, and equipment. At the same time, Barry Brady was named executive vice president of administration and Chuck Cianciaruso became vice president of marketing and preconstruction services.

The youngest of Bill Dunn's sons, Bob, had worked several summers during his high school and college years as a laborer and carpenter's apprentice for J.E. Dunn. After finishing his undergraduate degree in 1982, he worked in the safety department for Kansas City Power & Light, was a loan officer trainee for Centerre Bank, and pursued an MBA at Rockhurst. He would return to construction in a few years time.

A Downtown Landmark

*B*uilding was booming since the economy had emerged from the recession in late 1982. In the middle of the boom, J.E. Dunn embarked on the most ambitious project in its history – the AT&T Town Pavilion – with Bernard Jacquinot and Chuck Cianciaruso serving as project managers. The 38-story office building and retail mall would include renovation of surrounding buildings while swallowing an entire city

The AT&T Town Pavilion, the tallest building J.E. Dunn had ever built, represented many aspects of the company's growing business. The overall project, negotiated with AT&T on the strength of an existing relationship, was an example of a complex design/build approach relying on the teamwork of the owner, the architects and engineers – Howard, Needles, Tammen, and Bergendoff – and the general contractor. In addition, AT&T's several ancillary projects, including the construction of a clean room in Lee's Summit, and the renovation of the historic Boley and Harzfeld's buildings and their integration into the Town Pavilion complex, rendered it a model of construction management. In this type of project, the general contractor works in a supervisory capacity as well as that of a general contractor, ensuring that all elements of the project flow together smoothly for maximum cost-effectiveness and efficiency.

Those ancillary projects represented two significant and rapidly growing niches of J.E. Dunn's business in the 1980s: high-tech construction and renovation or retrofitting of historic structures. Fifteen years before, the AT&T project would likely not have included a clean room, and the Harzfeld and Boley buildings would have been bulldozed.

Because of its size, nature, and location, the AT&T Town Pavilion included a host of classic difficulties, including keeping to a tight schedule and building in tight spaces. To solve the tight space problem, a tractor-trailer was kept on full-time duty to move materials to the site. Hauling materials upward involved the use of a tower crane, seven personnel hoists, and three stiff-leg derricks.

The AT&T Town Pavilion represented the first time that J.E. Dunn dealt with the core of a project – stairs, elevators, shafts, and lobby – being slipformed. The Sundt Company was brought in to handle the effort, in which all core parts were produced in 10 weeks during the winter, and then installed quickly on-site, expediting the process by months.

Elmer Bishop was the general superintendent in charge of the tower, and Bill Miller was the general superintendent in charge of all retail floors. At completion, the AT&T Town Pavilion consisted of 1.2 million square feet and cost $115 million.

The AT&T Town Pavilion commands a prominent place in the Kansas City skyline.

block in downtown Kansas City, Mo. It would connect to nearby structures and garages by a series of bridges. A project of AT&T's real estate and office management division, the massive structure would house over 3,500 AT&T personnel in 930,000 square feet, and stores and restaurants in 210,000 square feet of retail space.

By Thanksgiving of 1986, two years and two months after ground was broken, J.E. Dunn brought the building in on budget and on time. It towered above the city skyline, a column of glass and steel serving as a beacon for urban dwellers. Unfortunately, three ironworkers working for a subcontractor lost their lives in its construction. Investigators found J.E. Dunn blameless in all three deaths. Dusty Strader, an ironworker foreman who labored on the project in his fourth decade with J.E. Dunn, was, like many, awed by the aesthetics, but mindful of the cost in labor and life. "The price was high and it was paid in full," he said. "The Town Pavilion, with the beauty of a woman, has the soul of an ironworker."

A Commitment to Safety

*I*n the construction industry, triumphs, in the form of successfully completed buildings are the norm, tragedies are rare, but near misses are common. A perfect example occurred in 1984, the year the AT&T Town Pavilion project started. On a cold snowy January morning, J.E. Dunn carpenter Jesse Hunt Jr. was working in a deep excavation on the site of the 16-story Plaza West office complex when he heard a crash, followed by the sound of grinding metal. He looked up and saw a 30-ton crane begin to tip toward him.

Jesse dropped his tools and scrambled down the ditch and up the side, slipping on the ice and snow in his haste. Seconds after vacating the area, he saw the crane operator leap to safety from the listing cab. The crane toppled off its moorings and into the excavation, landing on its top and badly bending the hydraulic boom arm.

No one was hurt, and it was later determined that melting ice caused the crane's metal pads to slip off the wooden pads that had been added for additional support.

Incidents like that reinforced J.E. Dunn's commitment to safety.

J.E. Dunn possessed an excellent safety record and a very low EMR, or Experience Modification Rating, which is given to all contractors by the National Council on Compensation Insurance based on cumulative loss experience for the previous three years. Still, J.E. Dunn wanted to improve upon its safety program. Safety director Steve Dunn hired Jim D. Miller, an engineer from the Office of Safety and Health Administration (OSHA), as an assistant in his office.

"Before I worked for Dunn," Miller said, "I was using them as a benchmark…so that just kind of shows you the credibility that Dunn had." Miller was soon promoted to assistant safety director, and eventually took over as safety director.

It took a bit of strong-arming from the top to impress upon all field personnel that safety, already the highest of priorities at J.E. Dunn, would be bulked up even more. "A lot of the older superintendents used to say 'we can't afford to do that, we didn't budget any money for that,'" reports Miller. "Well, we had a little problem on a job site one time, and I remember Mr. Dunn called every superintendent in to the office. We're sitting there and, boy, when Mr. Dunn talks, it's like a 500-pound gorilla! He says, 'a lot of you will go out and you'll be asked to do things and maybe you don't have it in your budget. I'll write you a personal check if I have to, but don't *ever* use that as an excuse for not doing something safe.' "

Safety, of course, also has a very practical side. "The safety record has had a big impact on our cost of doing business," says Steve Dunn. "We have some control on our cost for workers' comp insurance because that cost…takes into consideration the frequency of accidents and their severity over the three prior years. That's one reason that safety is so important, because if you can cut down on the frequency and cost of accidents, you'll…make the workers' comp insurance cheaper. Cheaper workers' comp costs may determine whether or not you're the low bidder on a job. But far more importantly, we have a moral obligation to provide a safe working environment for our employees."

Safety also matters to potential clients. "A lot of owners are insisting that you have a top-notch safety program," Steve says. "If you're going to do work for the Fortune 500 firms, they are extremely concerned about your safety program."

The Plaza West office building, where J.E. Dunn workers narrowly escaped injury from a falling crane.

BUSINESS BOOMS IN MID-DECADE

Construction Management: Guiding the School District in Rebuilding the Schools

*T*he Kansas City School District's expansion program represented one of the most significant projects of the mid-1980s and early 1990s.

The project sprang from a controversial court order requiring desegregation. School officials feared that forced busing might cause many parents to take their children from the public school system into private schools. They decided to compete for students by revamping the public schools.

For J.E. Dunn, the project became a $450 million example of construction management. Instead of contracting to build, J.E. Dunn would provide professional services in programming and project management, including the development of a comprehensive

procedure manual. The Capital Improvements Program, as it became known, ultimately involved the renovation of over 50 schools and the construction of 22 new ones. It included hundreds of contracts to consultants and general contractors.

Project Manager David Disney succeeded in maintaining budgets, quality control, and completion dates. "The Kansas City Missouri School District Capital Improvements Program was a turning point," says David, "because construction management had been used

Under the supervision of J.E. Dunn project manager, David Disney (below left), public school districts in the Kansas City area got a new look. The Independence School District authorized the construction of several new schools including the George Caleb Bingham 7th Grade Center (left). J.E. Dunn also supervised when the Garfield Elementary School in Kansas City was renovated (below).

in private projects, but never before on the public side of the equation." Under David's supervision, J.E. Dunn built on the effort with future projects for school districts such as Shawnee Mission in Kansas; North Kansas City, Mo.; Kansas City, Kan.; Salina, Kan.; Independence, Mo.; Platte County, Mo.; Denver; and Lincoln, Neb. David Disney is now a senior vice president who has overseen nearly $2 billion worth of construction management projects.

Finding A Niche: Specialty Building and Expansion

*W*hile the Town Pavilion and the Kansas City School District represented great achievements, Tulsa and Denver ultimately proved to be less than successful. "When Met Life decided to get out of real estate operations," says Bill Sr., "it soon became apparent that we were not planted as firmly in the Tulsa market as we needed to be if we were to take root." After facing uphill battles against hometown builders, the Tulsa office was closed just four years after it had opened. Mike Barr returned to Kansas City, where he is now senior vice president in charge

An interior view of the correctional facilities at the Wyandotte County Justice Complex in Kansas City, Kan.

of estimating at J.E. Dunn Construction. The Tulsa failure was not Barr's fault; J.E. Dunn had simply not yet found the correct formula for expansion.

The Denver office fared no better than Tulsa. The building boom that had prevailed in 1982 dissipated quickly, vacancies were high, and J.E. Dunn's contacts were as thin as they were in Tulsa. When the new executive also proved not to be a good fit with the company, that office was also closed. Dan Euston, now a senior vice president and division head for J.E. Dunn, and Dan West, currently a

J.E. Dunn vice president, cut their teeth in the tough Denver market. But the first grand experiment in expansion was over in less time than it took to build some major buildings.

Despite the struggles out of town, there was no lack of local activity to keep the company busy; while new cities had not proved fruitful, new areas of construction seemed more promising. After completing the Jackson County

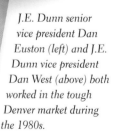

J.E. Dunn senior vice president Dan Euston (left) and J.E. Dunn vice president Dan West (above) both worked in the tough Denver market during the 1980s.

Correctional Facility in 1984, J.E. Dunn garnered a contract for the Western Missouri Correctional Center at Cameron, completed in 1988, and the Wyandotte County Justice Complex, completed in 1989. These projects were the first in a string of over 30 correctional institutions representing nearly a billion dollars of construction work.

The Western Missouri prison project presented a spate of problems typical for correctional facility construction. J.E. Dunn built a complete mock-up of one of the cells it would have to replicate many times over. The mock-up included reinforced masonry walls, a concrete slab floor, plumbing, wiring, furnishings, a door, and windows. Unlike a simple hotel room, however, the security issues for a prison cell required far more complex systems.

"We found some problems with the mock-up that we were able to correct before building the 1000 units," says Chris Sorensen, now assistant vice president. "In fact, the mock-up helped us create a cohesive coordination plan for the entire project."

Coordination and planning were particularly critical at Western Missouri for the electronic lock system on the 1,000-plus security doors. It required special wrenches, and all the doors had to be hung in sequence and coordinated with a centralized computer system. Because of its distance from a community of any size, Western Missouri required the construction of a 500,000-gallon water tower and an electrical substation.

By the end of the decade J.E. Dunn was becoming recognized for building correctional institutions.

A New Department, New Directors

*A*s the volume of construction work grew, J.E. Dunn decided to create a separate estimating department, headed by Mike Barr.

Also near the end of the 1980s, Bob Long, previously the senior managing partner at Arthur Andersen, was brought into Dunn Equities to manage the company's continued interests in expansion, despite the failures in Tulsa and Denver. He was charged with, in his words, "diversifying the equity into areas unrelated to construction business."

"We bought a percentage of J&M sportswear, which sold T-shirts and hats," says Barry Brady, by then head of Dunn Industries and hence Long's boss. "We had an investment in a bank holding company, along with the Hall family. We invested in real estate partnerships with DST in downtown office buildings. I don't think we lost money on anything. In fact, we probably made some money. But we really didn't know those businesses," he recounts.

While the experiment didn't prove to be as unproductive as the geographical expansion of the early 1980s, Long says the company decided to throw in the towel on most of this kind of expansion as well. "We decided, 'let's stick with what we know,'" he says. With the exception of a few partnered real estate investments, J.E. Dunn has not ventured out of the construction industry since.

Closing out the administrative restructuring of the decade, Bill Sr. chose to step down from day-to-day management in 1989. Barry Brady was made chief executive officer of Dunn Industries, making him essentially number two in the company behind Bill Sr. Terry was promoted to chief executive officer at J.E. Dunn Construction.

A new Paseo High School was made possible by the Capital Improvements Program in Kansas City, Mo. J.E. Dunn served as construction manager on physical improvement projects throughout the Kansas City, Missouri School District.

Lawyers and Greyhounds

*T*he end of the 1980s was a very exciting period marked by some exceptional projects.

The Shook Hardy & Bacon job, an eight-floor, 164,000 square foot renovation for a law firm, had to be completed in six months.

"Time was of the essence," says then project manager and now senior vice president Dirk Schafer, "because Shook Hardy & Bacon's lease detailed an exact start date for rent payments to begin." The tight schedule was particularly demanding given the large amount of highly detailed finish. More than five miles of wood base, 4,000 square feet of paneling, 82 wood columns, and 1,000 wood doors added up to one of the largest millwork projects in J.E. Dunn's history.

The wood, the highest quality grain veneer known as 'sapele pomele,' grows only in Africa. A single tree can be worth a million dollars, and armed guards protect the trees as they are floated down rivers to markets. J.E. Dunn received the wood as finished paneling, and it was installed by 35 carpenters selected for their reputations for quality craftsmanship. In addition to the wood, Shook Hardy & Bacon selected marbles of various colors for their eight elevator lobbies.

The Woodlands Racetrack and Kennel Club was another complex job. The $52 million project involved not only the tracks, but two grandstands and 53 separate buildings including kennel buildings, horse stables with jockey quarters, a test barn, and a maintenance building. Four million cubic yards of dirt were moved, making it the largest excavation job in Kansas City history after the Kansas City International Airport. The project was unique in that J.E. Dunn had to learn about a variety of sport-specific technologies: pari-mutuel machines (over 500 were wired for the two grandstands), closed-circuit sound and television systems, the tote board, the lure rail system with the mechanical rabbit that entices the dogs around the track, and a variety of other racing-specific technologies.

The most distinctive aspect of the project, however, was the fact that J.E. Dunn was given only nine months to complete the job.

The fast-track construction plan began with a creative and flexible labor agreement, eventually known as the Kansas City Works Plan, which Bill Sr. worked out with the Building and Construction Trades Council. The plan, which prohibited strikes, walkouts, or stoppages for any reason, including expiration of union contracts, centered on a rolling 40-hour work schedule. This allowed the first crew to work four ten-hour days before being relieved by the second crew, thus creating a continuous work force without any down days from beginning to end. There was no overtime except for holidays.

Bob Doran, president of Capital Electric, the electrical contractor for the Woodlands project, provides the perspective from the subcontractor's point of view. "When we were doing the Woodlands Dog Track, we showed J.E. Dunn what needed to happen to make the fixed schedule. The J.E. Dunn project people listened to us and bought into our schedule. Because J.E. Dunn let us do things our way, we finished 10 days ahead of schedule."

The Kansas City Works Plan allowed for twice as many workers on the ground as normal, and underscored the company's strong relationship with organized labor. It assured that the project would go on as scheduled without any work stoppages and yet maintain the quality union workmanship that was necessary to complete the project.

An Eye to Expansion

*B*y 1990, what had been one company was now four companies under the umbrella of Dunn Industries: J.E. Dunn Construction of Kansas City, the Dunn Family Foundation, Dunn Realty, and Dunn Equities. Two out-of-town subsidiaries had been closed, as had involvements with a variety of non-construction businesses. Bill Dunn Sr. had handed day-to-day responsibility over to Barry Brady, Steve Dunn, and Terry Dunn.

Losing some ground in the recession, the company had revenues of $155 million in 1990, making it the 247th largest general contractor in the U.S., according to *Engineering News Record* rankings.

As the last decade of the millennium dawned, J.E. Dunn was poised for continued growth. Undaunted by their mediocre record of expansion, the new leaders of J.E. Dunn were intent on spreading their wings beyond the confines of Kansas City.

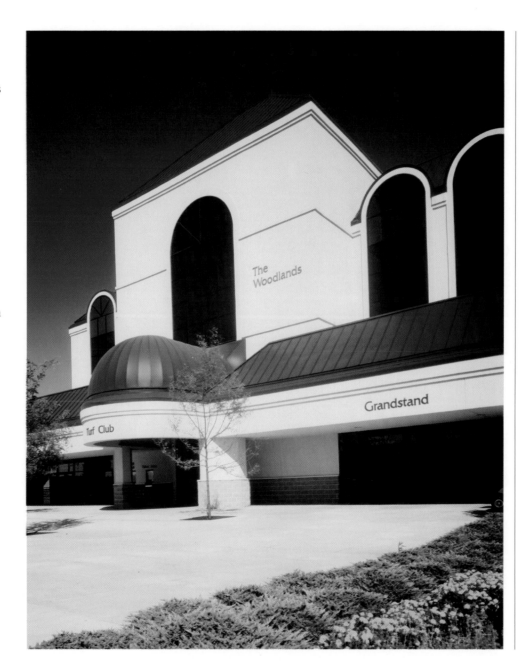

The Woodlands Racetrack and Kennel Club was completed in nine months with the help of construction crews working 10-hour days, seven days a week.

Chapter 6
STRETCHING FROM COAST TO COAST
1991-2003

Union Station, restored by
J.E. Dunn to its former glory.

CLOSING OUT THE TWENTIETH CENTURY

A Multi-Faceted Company

WITH 1,200 PEOPLE IN THE FIELD AND OFFICE, AND THE LION'S SHARE OF THE MAJOR LOCAL CONSTRUCTION PROJECTS PLANNED OR UNDERWAY, J.E. DUNN WAS THE PREMIER GENERAL CONTRACTOR IN THE KANSAS CITY AREA IN 1990.

J.E. Dunn provided its clients with exemplary preconstruction and construction management services. These services were important for school districts, Shawnee Mission in Kansas, North Kansas City, Mo., and Kansas City, Kan., where complex projects often involved multiple buildings or sites, and allowed the company, according to David Disney, "to establish new relationships with architects and other contractors." Basic construction, however, remained the core of the business, and the company

(above) Overland Trail Middle School, for the Blue Valley School District in Kansas.

(right) A broad sweep of windows gives students a panoramic view in the library at Park Hill South High School, a J.E. Dunn project in Kansas City's Northland area.

maintained a particularly strong reputation for building hospitals, schools, hotels, office buildings, and public facilities such as courthouses and prisons.

J.E. Dunn's diversification also protected it against inevitable cycles in individual market sectors. As a result, the economic downturn of the late 1980s was less challenging for J.E. Dunn than those of 1974 and 1980-82. For example, a significant drop during that period in commercial building, the result of overbuilding and the Tax Reform Act of 1986, was offset by an increase in industrial, housing, and institutional work.

New Opportunities: Civil, Environmental, High-Tech

New opportunities continued to arise. Government mandates to clean up waterways brought environmental work to J.E. Dunn, such as the $13.6 million construction of a sludge treatment facility for the Little Blue Valley Sewer District in Jackson County, Mo., and the $15.8 million Big Blue River wastewater treatment plant for the city of Kansas City, Mo. New projects, however, always require a learning curve, and Lou Hilker calls

Big Blue one of the most difficult projects of his career. The project had complex de-watering systems that involved pumping up to 15 million gallons of water per day out of the construction area throughout the life of the project.

Privatized correctional facilities also brought new opportunities and partnerships. Privatization eliminated the need for public debt by replacing taxes or bonds, the traditional funding mechanisms, with investment from large financial institutions, often reducing costs by 15 to 20 percent in the process. The Leavenworth Detention Center, a J.E. Dunn project in the early-1990s, was the first facility ever built and operated for the U.S. Marshals Service by the private sector. Corrections Corporation of America, the lead partner at Leavenworth, called it "an unprecedented step between the government and private industry to help solve the growing shortage of space for federal pre-trial detainees."

The burgeoning high-tech industry opened another market for J.E. Dunn. Terms like "clean rooms" and "data centers" became part of the builder's lexicon.

J.E. Dunn had actually gotten its feet wet with high-tech construction as early as 1980 with a three-story addition to the Farmland Data Processing Center. Though the project involved only

(top) An aerial view of the Big Blue Waste Water Facility.

(bottom) The Sludge Disposal Building at the Little Blue Valley Sewer District.

Working in tight spaces is one of the challenges of urban construction. The surrounding streets and blocks where people walk and drive are often compromised by a project as materials, equipment, and hundreds of construction workers enter and exit the site.

A tight work area was a problem in the construction of the AT&T Town Pavilion, so 120 days prior to construction, J.E. Dunn created a mobilization plan that diagrammed where hoists, cranes, and derricks would be located to move people and materials vertically during construction, and how truck traffic would flow through the site. While developing and implementing these plans, J.E. Dunn worked in cooperation with the city to close sidewalks and streets, restrict vehicular traffic, and to set up fences, gates, and security systems.

The Mutual Benefit Life Building, an 11-story concrete building with four levels of parking below ground, was constructed at about the same time. Not only was it a tight site just a few feet from the existing Mutual Benefit office tower, but as project manager Dirk Schafer explains, there were other issues. "Because of the depth and breadth of the excavation and its close proximity to surrounding buildings, bridges, and streets, an extensive and innovative excavation

plan was employed to blast through thick layers of limestone and shale."

J.E. Dunn conducted a pre-blast survey consisting of thousands of photographs of all structures nearby, documenting every pre-blast crack and imperfection. It used a blasting consultant and two seismographs, and computed the maximum Peak Particle Velocity with increasingly powerful test blasts to ascertain that the blasts would not disturb the surrounding structures.

Dirk Schafer served as project manager during construction of the Mutual Benefit Life building at left above.

16,000 square feet, J.E. Dunn learned the special requirements for facilities housing computers and data systems, and the need for keeping facilities operational at all times throughout construction.

A few years later, the AT&T Computer Center at Lee's Summit, Mo., required interior remodeling for its clean room where computer chips were produced. Demolition of existing structures preceded installation of special utility connections, special gas systems, and a sophisticated computer temperature/humidity control system to ensure a proper climate for delicate construction of microelectronics. The project entailed over 60 different bid packages from different subcontractors.

DST's Winchester Data Center in Kansas City was built around the same time as the AT&T Computer Center. An 83,000 square foot addition would be added to DST Winchester in 1994. According to project manager, and now senior vice president Dan Euston, "this time we were working around a fully functioning data center." The requirement for DST to never go off-line demanded numerous redundant power systems and a direct tie-in to Kansas City Power & Light's substation as the main power source. A special uninterruptible power source served the cooling system and

High-tech jobs like the Blue Cross and Blue Shield Data Center in Topeka became a staple for J.E. Dunn in the 1980s.

kept the computers operating at peak efficiency. In the event of a direct tornado hit, the precast panels on the outside of the building were designed to crumble like safety glass, and a double-roofing system was designed so the top roof could be blown entirely off while a sub-roof would remain to protect the contents of the building.

In the late 1980s, Blue Cross and Blue Shield in Topeka conceived of "a gigantic, high-tech 'boat' in the middle of a parking lot," as they explained it to J.E. Dunn. A 123,400 square foot, four-story data center located half underground, the structure had to be entirely waterproof. A very tight space and the need to share a driveway with two other office buildings added to the complexity

of the project, and required detailed scheduling so as not to interrupt existing operations. To ensure protection from underground water seepage, J.E. Dunn built numerous redundant protections around the foundation walls and under the foundation slab.

By the 1990s, when Boatmen's Bank wanted a new 96,700 square foot data center, J.E. Dunn was almost as adept at high-tech building as it was with hospitals and other specialty construction. Boatmen's data center was particularly challenging, however, because the bank wanted it to be up and running in nine months so that it could take advantage of the three-day Martin Luther King Jr. holiday for transferring banking data.

(right) J.E. Dunn consulted with staff doctors and nurses using mock-ups of patient rooms before construction at Bryan Memorial Hospital in Lincoln, Neb.

(bottom) As general contractor at Swope Parkway Health Center, J.E. Dunn gave 47 percent of its subcontracted work to minority-owned firms and 7 percent to firms owned by women.

"If we missed the deadlines, the cost to delay the project would be in the millions of dollars," said then senior project manager Jeff Campbell, now an assistant vice president. Boatmen's Data Center tied together all the data and ATM machines in a nine state area, and, like other data centers, had to remain running at all times. Again, redundant systems, structures that could withstand both natural and man-made disasters, and uninterruptible power sources were all required. On moving day, when all the equipment and truckloads of magnetic tape were scheduled to be moved from Boatmen's old data center in St. Louis to Kansas City, the prospect of a major snowstorm threatened the entire operation. Fortunately, the weather held off, the trucks made it through, and Boatmen's made their deadline.

Difficult Projects Abound

*H*igh-tech projects were not the only difficult assignments. With such a varied assortment of building projects, challenges would continue to come in all forms and sizes throughout the 1990s.

J.E. Dunn completed the Citicorp Credit Collection Center in Kansas City, Mo., in 1997.

Despite the many successes and many technological advances, construction remained a dangerous endeavor in the 1990s.

In 1994, J.E. Dunn was engaged to build an expansion onto DST's Winchester Data Center, and at about 9:30 a.m. on October 19, a cable from a crane touched a high voltage power line. Over 160,000 volts immediately traveled down the line to the ground and spread out, shocking five men who were standing within 25 feet. All five were sent to the hospital and released, with no serious injuries resulting.

A much more serious accident that happened in February 1996 struck close to home. Terry Dunn's brother-in-law, Joe Clune, was working as an operating engineer for J.E. Dunn on the renovation of the New York Life Building in downtown Kansas City, when he died after falling nine stories down a temporary elevator shaft. It was a terrible tragedy and J.E.Dunn's first job-related death in many years.

In construction, the potential for accidents is high. The only hope is to keep working toward better site safety standards. Jim Miller, J.E. Dunn's safety director, says, "I am kind of proud of our OSHA history. If you look over the last 14-15 years, I could probably count the number of times we have been cited on one hand. And we have been inspected hundreds of times. So, our OSHA inspection history is excellent."

(left) An interior view of the New York Life Building after its renovation.

(right) Jim D. Miller, J.E. Dunn safety director.

Superintendent Jay Lucas says that of all the challenges, short time frames and tenant finish operations represented the biggest concerns. "The worst jobs," he says, "are those with tough schedules. You get worn down. There has been a change in the way of thinking. It used to be once you turned over the key, you were done. Now we give [the owners] buildings two months before we're done. Now we are working amongst them."

Tight timelines kept popping up on J.E. Dunn's calendar. In late 1991 the Bryan Memorial Hospital in Lincoln, Neb., was a $53 million project due to be finished in only three years; in1993 the Citicorp building was given a tight, one-year timeline; and the Western Missouri prison, begun in 1995, was also on a tight schedule. Jacobson's Department Store, a 120,000 square foot anchor store for an upscale shopping mall in Leawood, Kan., required an exceptionally fast-track schedule to meet its spring 1996 opening. J.E. Dunn was only given eight months on a project that should have taken at least ten.

The biggest challenge in tightly scheduled projects lies in coordinating different deadlines for deliveries and subcontractors. At Jacobson's J.E. Dunn divided the building into different construction zones, each with their own schedule. "By working in zones," says then project manager, now senior vice president Mike Householder, "we were able to totally complete departments and have them ready for merchandise while we were still hanging drywall in adjacent areas." It was a fast-track approach that enabled J.E. Dunn to meet the aggressive deadline.

Minority Participation

Minority participation has always been important for J.E. Dunn. For example, in 1995 J.E. Dunn was able to award 47 percent of its subcontracts to minority firms and 7 percent to women-owned firms for the construction of Swope Parkway Health Center.

Finding minority subcontractors is not always easy. Aware of the pressure to hire minorities, some unscrupulous companies will use front people when in fact the minority personnel are not given any management responsibility.

Jack Steadman of Hunt Enterprises puts J.E. Dunn's practice of hiring minority firms in historical perspective: "There was a time when a city councilman was attacking Bill Sr. for not getting enough minority participation on construction jobs, when Bill was trying as hard as he

The spacious auditorium at the RLDS (now Community of Christ) Temple in Independence, Mo.

The nautilus-inspired tower at the RLDS Temple spirals skyward.

could. A lot of people would have run from that, but Bill was never perturbed. He just kept plugging away, plugging away, and now he has developed a large contingent of minorities who are qualified construction people…"

Paul Rodriguez, a Hispanic mechanical subcontractor who has worked on J.E. Dunn projects for most of the 1990s, says that Dunn is not simply putting on a show for public or minority-related projects. "Dunn is all about including people," he says. "They believe in equal opportunity and diversity."

In fact, Ray Malone, an African-American and president of Malco Steel, goes on to note that establishing good relationships with subcontractors has not solely been a minority issue, but a broader professional, or even humane one. "I have seen [J.E. Dunn] time and time again, when subcontractors were on the verge of going out of business, pay invoices early just to keep the subcontractors in business," he says. "They have hired professional consultants to help minority and women businesses keep going."

RLDS Temple

*B*eing inclusive in its labor force took on a new dimension for J.E. Dunn in 1994 when it began building

Beads of light shine down on the interior of the RLDS Temple.

the $35 million temple at the world headquarters of the Reorganized Church of Jesus Christ of Latter Day Saints (now known as the Community of Christ) in Independence, Mo. J.E. Dunn granted the church's request to allow church members to work alongside its own crews on the project.

The temple, with its unique nautilus-shaped tower, represented one of the most unusual and challenging designs J.E. Dunn had ever faced. According to Bishop Norm Swails, then presiding bishop of the RLDS community, the designers, Hellmuth, Obata & Kassebaum "came up

with the spiral as a universal symbol that appears in nature – the seashell – because it is never-ending, always changing, and never the same. The spiral is different every way you look at it, and the idea is that humanity, at its best, works toward the divine, but the divine also spreads through the world."

At first there was concern that the tower couldn't even be built as designed. The diminishing size of the spiral meant that it could not be constructed in standard repetitive sections. Utilizing three-dimensional drawings and CAD software, the tower was broken into 24 different design segments. Inside the structure, 24 steel beams zigzag upward and inward every 15 degrees from the base to the top, 208 feet above the ground. As in other complex projects, J.E. Dunn relied on peer review to verify the engineering design.

To build this unique structure, J.E. Dunn used a temporary internal shoring tower to provide support for the steel framework sections. When the shoring tower was cut loose and removed from the completed tower, the building only moved ⅛ inch.

For general superintendent Rick Fortner, it was one of the first projects in which he had been involved in the team concept between owner, architect,

and builder. "I enjoyed that project a lot. It could have been the most difficult but it was one of the best. It just went great. We had a good owner and a smooth job. The owner and architect were involved in everything, and there were no surprises. It was the first job for me where the owner was involved and where it was the team concept. Now it is typical where we create a bond with the people."

Despite its complexity, the tower represented only one of the challenges. For instance, to meet a nearly impossible deadline for a parking lot, which was to be used for a benefit at the owner's nearby auditorium, J.E. Dunn arranged for six self-propelled curbing machines instead of one, and finished the project in three days instead of the nearly three weeks it would have taken.

Bishop Swails was grateful, and recognized the unique aspects of the job. "Through their influence with the unions, they did two things that are generally impossible. One, they allowed us to have some volunteer people on the site, giving preferential employment to any church member from anywhere in the country that came with skills and wanted a job to work on the temple. And two, they got their unions and trades people to enforce no-smoking, no-tobacco, no-alcohol, no-drugs, and

Assistant Vice President Martin Blood began developing conceptual estimating software for J.E. Dunn in 1988.

Estimating comes in two forms – negotiated and hard bid jobs.

Negotiated work represents 80 percent of J.E. Dunn's business over the past thirty years. J.E. Dunn's preconstruction services, such as early cost analysis, quality assurance, critical path scheduling, and value engineering, can save an owner from 15 to 20 percent on a job.

Conceptual estimating – being able to evaluate how much a project will cost before the construction plans are complete and sometimes before there are any plans at all – is another preconstruction service that gives J.E. Dunn an edge in both the negotiated and hard bid arenas. Martin Blood, a longtime J.E. Dunn employee and its first full-time estimator, gets much of the credit

for the company's expertise in conceptual estimating and for bringing the estimating department into the computer age. In 1988, he began developing conceptual estimating software, using earlier J.E. Dunn jobs for his cost data base. He continues to oversee its evolution.

Despite all the advances in estimating software, hard bid jobs continue to bring their share of stress to the estimating department. Bidding requires an intense commitment of manpower for three to six weeks. After the estimators determine the scope of the work, they must decide the types of subcontractors needed and evaluate their financial capabilities. The estimating team will construct the entire project on paper.

Coordinating likely subcontractor schedules and scheduling materials based on availability is part of the bidding process. If possible, the owner is involved so he can answer questions about his plans.

Ultimately, as many as 500 letters go out requesting bids from subcontractors.

"Bid day can be controlled chaos with 200 bids coming in within a two to three hour period," says Mike Barr, senior vice president in charge of estimating. The "Do Not Disturb" sign goes up on the door in the northwest corner room at the J.E. Dunn offices on Holmes, and people almost tiptoe past as all the numbers are crunched before the witching hour.

The goal, of course, is to submit a bid lower than any of the competitors while still achieving a reasonable profit on the work. If the bid is too low, the company may win the job but lose money.

"Sometimes it all comes together in the last two to three minutes," says Mike Barr. "It is a test of a contractor's organizational and management skills."

no-foul language policies. When the trucks would drive in, someone would be there ready to enforce these rules."

Expansion

*A*s the CEO of J.E. Dunn Construction, Terry Dunn maintained his long-standing priority: growth through expansion. The things he considered failures in the 1980s – geographical expansion to Tulsa and Denver, and expansion into different industries – were lessons along the way.

By the time J.E. Dunn was ready to try again, the company had developed a new approach to avoid getting "hometowned." "We learned our lesson, and I think it's been a very good lesson ever since," says Bill Sr. "As we go into a new area we have found it works much better to acquire an existing company."

After closing the Tulsa and Denver offices, J.E. Dunn looked elsewhere for an established company. They found it in Minneapolis, with the almost 50-year-old Dean L. Witcher Construction Company. Established just after World War II as a concrete and masonry subcontractor, Witcher had expanded into general construction, with an emphasis on retail work throughout Minnesota and the Dakotas. Founder Dean Witcher had

passed away in 1968, and now owner Mike Redmond was looking to reduce his involvement in the business. "I helped on the due diligence, investigating whether it was a good investment," said Terry. "We bought 51 percent of the company."

From the beginning, J.E. Dunn learned the problems of merging corporate cultures. "We learned early on after the purchase that our companies were different," says Terry.

In 1994, the involvement with Witcher increased when Mike Redmond was injured in an auto accident and had to sell the other 49 percent of his company. Terry Dunn notes that the difficulties in Minneapolis continued. "When we bought Redmond out we found that Witcher did not have a strong relationship with major clients. For about a year many customers decided to back away from doing business with Witcher, so we were at a major financial disadvantage. Then we made the right decision to promote Ken Styrlund of Witcher to president and since that time Witcher Construction Co. has been a success. They now emphasize retail, churches, and multi-family housing construction."

Ultimately, Witcher, which had always practiced excellent construction, had to include a focus on clients among its

priorities. "Witcher had always had an outstanding field operation," says Terry. "Now their treatment of customers is similar to ours. We were able to win back clients who'd done business with Witcher previously. It's been a very nice evolution."

Terry credits much of the success of Witcher Construction Co., now known as J.E. Dunn-North Central, to the work done by Ken Styrlund. "Ken has done an excellent job. Under his direction, the company has grown from a $20 million-a-year operation to grossing anywhere from $120 to $150 million annually. He's led an outstanding group of quality people."

In 1992, between its first and second purchases of Witcher, J.E. Dunn bought the Drake Construction Company in Portland, Ore. Founded in 1921, Drake was about the same age as J.E. Dunn Construction. A major general contractor with annual revenues of about $90 million, Drake had worked for U.S. Bancorporation and the University of Oregon Health Services. Significantly bigger than Witcher, the Drake acquisition held out high hopes for both companies. J.E. Dunn soon discovered, however, that, as with Witcher, Drake had an uneasy relationship with existing clients. Fred Shipman, who had come to J.E. Dunn in the 1970s and was now an executive vice president, was sent to

Drake to become president and CEO and to foster the J.E. Dunn culture. His success is evident in Drake's subsequent productivity and increased repeat and referral business. The Portland company changed its name to J.E. Dunn-Northwest in 1999, and added an office in Seattle in 2001.

Shipman's departure for Portland also changed the structure of project management at J.E. Dunn back home in Kansas City. Division heads were created within the project management department.

Steve Hamline, Dan Euston, Mike Barr, Jim R. Miller, and David Disney served as the original division heads in Kansas City. While Miller specialized in health care projects and Disney's area of emphasis was in education, the others oversaw a variety of construction projects.

Division heads continued to be added over time. In 1997 Dirk Schafer was made a division head when he returned to J.E. Dunn after a stint with another construction company. Mike Barr left project management to devote more time to running the estimating department. Most recently, Mike Householder became a division head in Steve Hamline's division in 2002 when Steve went to head up J.E. Dunn's offices in Colorado Springs and Denver.

The J.E. Dunn office in Kansas City was redesigned and expanded during the early 1990s to make room for more employees. The new entrance on the north side of the building is pictured.

Senior Vice President Steve Hamline heads up the J.E. Dunn offices in Denver and Colorado Springs.

Steve Hamline believes the division head structure was a positive one for J.E. Dunn, commenting that "it really turned us loose to grow, and allowed independence for the division heads."

Dirk Schafer agrees, "The division head system gave me more autonomy, more responsibility, and much more opportunity." As a division head, Dirk sees business development as a major part of his job to help lay the groundwork for future projects for his division. He also emphasizes preconstruction services. "That's when we can have the greatest impact on the success of a job."

Division heads often oversee 10 to 15 projects at a time. To be effective at that task requires "someone capable of a lot of good preplanning and someone who can grasp the big picture," according to Mike Householder. "The job also means burning the midnight oil as you go over blueprints because there are so many other issues to deal with during the day."

PREPARING FOR A NEW CENTURY

Reorganization

*B*y the mid 1990s, prices overall had risen 20 percent in five years. Because of successful expansion, J.E. Dunn's revenues had outstripped that figure, growing 379 percent from $104 million in 1990 to $402 million in 1995. With an operation that suddenly stretched north to Canada and west to the Pacific, it was time once again to reexamine the administrative structure.

At the top of the list were the accounting systems which Arnold Dreyer and Dale Shikles had overhauled in the 1970s, and which had been computerized in the interim. "We hired Professional Systems Corporation to write our programs from scratch and we got a custom-made program to fit us at a very reasonable price," says Shikles. "It wouldn't be economically feasible to do that today. They gave us a good deal, one, because we were J.E. Dunn, and, two, because they spent more time on it than they estimated."

Senior Vice President Jim R. Miller leads J.E. Dunn's division specializing in health care construction.

Senior Vice President Mike Householder became a division head in 2002.

In 2000, a new logo was created to represent all the Dunn subsidiaries operating as one family of companies. "The new look will more closely reflect each company's link to a national organization – the J.E. Dunn Group," said Terry Dunn.

The company also made an adjustment to its procedure for returning savings to owners. Robert Berkebile, principal of BNIM Architects, with whom J.E. Dunn has worked closely on a number of projects, notes that, "years ago, Dunn would give a price to do a project and everyone would work hard, and in the end Dunn would hand the owner a large check for the project savings. This caused some problems because, in some cases, the customer would have liked to improve the building with this extra money instead of pocketing the savings. Now, there is a more collaborative effort to make sure the owner and the architect know where

the budget is as the project goes on. This allows us to get the best possible building for the project budget."

The biggest administrative change was the decision in 1999 to bring the first outside directors to Dunn Industries. "The thinking," says Bill Sr. "was that we were growing quickly and needed outside input from people who do their own thinking and are not rubber-stamped."

The first group of directors included William Hall, head of the Hall Family Foundation; Ed Matheny, one of the principals of Blackwell Sanders Matheny, a local law firm; Mike Morrissey who headed up Ernst and Young's office in Kansas City; Sandra Lawrence, an

executive with Gateway Computer; and Barry Brady, who had moved in 1998 from J.E. Dunn into the top executive position at the J.C. Nichols Company in Kansas City.

Bill Sr., Steve, Bill Jr., Terry, and Bob, along with their brother, Kevin Dunn (who has never worked at J.E. Dunn), and Bob Long, made up the rest of the board. This latter group of individuals, with Bernard Jacquinot in place of Kevin Dunn, also made up the J.E. Dunn Construction Company board.

In a departure from the practices of most family-owned businesses, the board made up partially of outsiders acted from the start not simply in an advisory capacity, but as a voting body heading up subcommittees and engaging in serious strategic planning. No conflicts between the board and the family have ever arisen because, according to Bill Dunn Sr., all parties are fairly homogenous and conservative. The board "has been a blessing, and I am grateful to Donald Hall, the chairman of Hallmark Cards, for his recommendation that we needed outside directors," he says.

Utilizing the board effectively is critical, says Bob Long, who is today the chairman of the Dunn Industries board. "We need to guard against the tendency to get them too involved in the day-to-day operations.

A curving stairway ascends the lobby of the Charles Evans Whittaker Federal Courthouse.

Bob Long (r), chairman of Dunn Industries, talks with Bill Dunn Sr.

We need to keep them up at the strategy and policy level because they do not have the day-to-day operational knowledge of our individual people and their abilities."

Long, however, does not question their impact and importance. "I think they bring a viewpoint that we need to hear," he says, "I think that the outside directors are an excellent source of objectivity. Their effectiveness is based solely on our being open and laying the problems before them and discussing our thoughts, our plans, our strategies."

More High-Profile Projects

*M*uch of the work that J.E. Dunn landed in the mid-1990s represents many of the signature buildings in Kansas City.

The 615,000 square foot Charles Evans Whittaker U.S. Courthouse helped revitalize the east side of downtown Kansas City. The courthouse was completed in September 1998 and houses 16 courtrooms, the Circuit Court of Appeals, U.S. Attorneys' office, U.S. Marshals' offices, judges' chambers, court-related agencies, extensive multimedia conferencing facilities, a cafeteria and

The Charles Evans Whittaker U.S. Courthouse in downtown Kansas City.

kitchen, and enclosed secured parking for 100 vehicles. A five-story rotunda at the center drives an overall circular design, which, above the rotunda, is open for the next five floors, like a cake with a slice removed. The design is more than creative, however, for it encompasses a system of stairways, halls, and elevators in which three distinct populations – judges, prisoners, and the public – move about without coming into contact.

As with the RLDS temple, the unusual design led to construction complexities. "The radius design is very unique and complicated," says Rick Fortner, the general superintendent on the project. "Everything is custom with very little repetition. Each floor has a different height because of the different courtroom designs."

The circular shape also demanded construction in triangular sections, again like slices of cake. Because of the lack of repetition, all the construction materials – steel, joists, everything – were cut to different lengths. To add to the complexity, a trade and competitiveness act signed by Congress in 1988 and passed into law in 1994 required all federal buildings to be constructed according to the metric system, rendering useless every ruler, tape measure, and manual referring only to feet and inches.

A company from Denver served as construction manager and brought together all parties – J.E. Dunn, the owner (General Services Administration), the tenant (U.S. Courts) and other involved parties – to partner in a joint mission statement. According to senior vice president Steve Hamline, this effort

"helped all involved maintain a positive attitude toward resolving any problems or potential problems in order to keep the project moving."

"We are using this process more and more," said J.E. Dunn Construction CEO Terry Dunn at the time, "and are 100 percent committed to partnering and building on client relationships." In 2001, J.E. Dunn received the Honor Award for Construction Excellence from the General Services Administration for its work on the Courthouse. The federal government had acknowledged J.E. Dunn a year earlier when the construction company received the 2000 U.S. Postal Service's Quality Supplier Award in the Large Business-Operational Services category for work it completed on a $48 million postal processing and distribution center in Kansas City.

The Stowers Institute for Medical Research represented another example of partnering, this time with a client with whom J.E. Dunn had worked before in building the two American Century Towers.

Jim Stowers, founder of American Century Investments, and his wife, Virginia, were both cancer survivors when they decided to commit their fortune to creating "the best biomedical research center in the world." Like many

ambitious dreams, the odds were stacked against it. The first concern centered around whether top scientists and medical personnel could be attracted to the heartland when most such research centers were on one of the coasts. A second involved the fact that the preferred 10-acre site was the home of the rambling, outdated Menorah Medical Center, which the Stowerses realized held an emotional connection for many in the local Jewish community.

From the J.E. Dunn perspective, Stowers was unusual in his commitment to achieving excellence without regard to price. When asked, "How much do you want to spend?" Jim Stowers replied, "Well, how much does it cost to do it right?"

Eventually a plan was conceived to retain roughly half the Menorah Medical complex, refurbish the old buildings, and construct a research center around them, which would outshine all other such centers across the nation in both amenities and luxury.

A 267,000 square foot research building in the heart of the Institute would draw on all J.E. Dunn's experience in high-tech construction. As described by *Impressions*, J.E. Dunn's newsletter, "vertical shafts were installed every 45 feet to carry natural gas, liquid nitrogen and other supplies to

(right) J.E. Dunn did extensive hardscaping on the grounds of the Nelson-Atkins Museum of Art in the early 1990s. A Henry Moore sculpture "reclines" in the foreground.

(below) Chrome and color brighten the Orbit's Diner at Childen's Mercy Hospital, another repeat client for J.E. Dunn.

In the long course of a project, satisfying the client takes on many different aspects, from saving money in the planning, to listening and communicating effectively, to working with architects and subcontractors.

Richard Hastings, chief executive officer of Saint Luke's Hospital, a J.E. Dunn project, relates his experiences with the construction company. "They have been good partners with us. Dunn does a really good job working with the architects by not being a threat to them, unlike a lot of contractors. Quality and commitment and expertise are the characteristics that make them successful."

Frank Devocelle, president of Olathe Health Systems, is appreciative of J.E. Dunn's specialized knowledge. "There is not a construction company around with the health care knowledge that Dunn has. This makes them the premier contractor for health care projects. Also their depth of knowledge allows them to contribute to the design as well as the construction of the building."

Shirley Helzberg, who has been involved with several not-for-profit J.E. Dunn projects, such as the additions for the Starlight Theater and the Nelson-Atkins Museum, speaks of more personal matters. "They treat you with great respect when you go on jobsites. I am so impressed with the knowledge they have about the different costs on a project. You get a lot of confidence in their knowledge. This is especially important when you are responsible for other people's money."

Success depends on reputation, and reputation depends on customer service and client satisfaction. Randall O'Donnell, president and CEO of Children's Mercy Hospitals and Clinics, believes J.E. Dunn's ability to put all the pieces together has translated into their overall success. "Dunn is a premier contractor who is responsible for my special needs. There is never a worry about safety or operations concerns. There is no guesswork about the end result. Projects are on time and within budget. They have no peer in the construction industry."

(opposite) The Stowers Institute puts Kansas City in the forefront of medical research.

After being neglected for decades, the Liberty Memorial was restored by J.E. Dunn in the late 1990s. More work is planned for the site.

each laboratory floor. Two laboratory floors were filled with crisscrossing ductwork, conduit, piping, and equipment."

"Basically, this is a big mechanical facility with some architecture wrapped around it,' " said Jeff Johnson, Stowers' owner's representative.

At its completion in November 2000, the $225 million research facility had 50 large laboratories, each capable of housing a team of scientists. Outstanding office, conference, and library facilities completed the package.

"Our main focus was centered on delivering a quality project as quickly as possible. The Stowers Institute was finished in two years within the owner's budget. We were committed to Mr. Stowers, and wanted to get it done for him," said Rick Fortner, J.E. Dunn general superintendent.

Mr. Stowers openly expressed his gratitude. "They build from the heart," he said. "Rick wanted to make sure everyone believed in what they were trying to do. 'Do it right the first time' was the motto. He put lots of signs up with mottos."

Bill Sr. has gone on record as saying he believes the Stowers Institute is one of the finest projects J.E. Dunn has ever built.

Just as J.E. Dunn relied upon its expertise in high-tech construction to fashion the Stowers Institute, so too did it depend upon its expertise of renovation and restoration to rebuild one of the jewels of downtown Kansas City – Union Station.

The renovation of the existing structure, which once numbered 900 rooms, included the 95-foot high ceiling in the Grand Hall, three 3,500-pound chandeliers, and a 6-foot wide clock hanging in the Station's central arch. Additional work involved a 60,000 square foot addition for a Science City Museum; a 225,000 square foot, 2-story parking garage; and a unique covered skywalk from the Westin Crown Center Hotel.

Twenty years of neglect had left Union Station with a leaky roof, rusted beams, and deteriorated plaster and flooring. It wouldn't be an easy renovation. A deck was constructed 82 feet above the floor

to allow work to proceed on the 90-foot high ceiling. Glass fiber-reinforced gypsum was used for ceiling moldings instead of plaster the second time around. Two experienced craftsmen worked for two weeks on the outside of the clock alone, and more craftsmen worked much longer restoring the internal working mechanisms. Five semi-tractor trailers carted away all the old light fixtures to St Louis, where they were restored to their original luster. Limestone was power-washed, cast-iron was re-bronzed with turn-of-the-century techniques, and an extensive search was made to find matching marble to repair the floor.

J.E. Dunn's general superintendent Harold Jansen oversaw the construction work at Union Station. Even though they were forced to take constant precautions against numerous hazardous substances, such as lead paint, asbestos, mercury, and bat droppings, the crew once again finished the job on time and under budget.

Jansen was also general superintendent when J.E. Dunn restored another historic site in Kansas City: the Liberty Memorial. The Liberty Memorial was built in 1926 as the nation's largest monument to World War I. Closed to the public in 1994 because of structural problems, largely from water damage undermining the deck and supporting

With 21 buildings, 220 acres of a former soybean field, four million square feet of office space, another four million square feet in 14 parking garages, and its own zip code, the Sprint World Headquarters Campus was the largest single office project ever constructed in the United States.

When J.E. Dunn was hired for the work, senior vice president Dan Euston started building the team that would include 20 on-site project managers, 10 additional clerical support and administrative personnel, and five general superintendents: David Ayres, Vern Orpin, Bill Harris, Terry Dlugosh, and Rusty Tuggle. A total of $100 million in contracts was awarded to women-owned and minority-owned subcontractors and suppliers.

Despite the many buildings, 60 percent of the campus was dedicated to green space – prairie grasses, flowers, trees, walking paths, jogging trails, and a lake, and yet it was all designed so that walking across campus would take no more than 10 minutes.

Great efficiencies were achieved in both design and purchasing. A "bulk buy" approach was used so certain materials were identified, standardized, and purchased ahead of scheduled delivery dates. Common building features, such as elevators, were standardized for streamlined maintenance. Frequently used materials were efficiently warehoused and pulled out of stock as needed, without guesswork or delivery delays.

The materials used were staggering: 250,000 cubic yards of concrete, 88 elevators, 72 air handlers, over 5,000 pieces of hardware, 1,569 toilets, 100 acres of carpet, 7.5 million bricks, and 15 cranes – including a new crane from Spain with a 243-foot radius.

For Dan Euston, however, the size was nothing special. "It's just a bigger project. The real benefit was the way the Sprint job has caused us to focus again on what's going on in the telecommunications industry."

(left) Water features course throughout the Sprint Campus.

(right) A clock tower, traditionally styled brick buildings, and large shade trees give the Sprint World Headquarters the look of a college campus.

(above) Senior vice president Gordon Lansford.

(right) An aerial view of the Sprint Campus.

columns under the tower, the memorial was due for a renovation of its own.

J.E. Dunn won the bidding on the $50 million taxpayer-funded project, returning to the site where the company had built a dedication wall during World War II.

Finally, the biggest project of the decade involved what J.E. Dunn senior vice president Dan Euston calls "the Super Bowl of Projects" – the Sprint World Headquarters Campus in Overland Park, Kan. Easily the largest project in the history of J.E. Dunn Construction, Sprint represented another massive team effort by the owner, designer, and J.E. Dunn, the general contractor and construction manager for the 200-acre, 18 building, 3.9 million square foot facility. Designed to look like a college campus dominated by a clock tower, the Sprint Campus required 40 superintendents and more than 1,200 construction personnel. When completed in 2002, it was the largest single-company office complex in the United States.

More Subsidiaries, New Marketing Strategies

*O*utside of Kansas City, Witcher and Drake were finally proving successful. It appeared J.E. Dunn had finally found the correct formula for expansion. "We developed a two-pronged strategy toward growth: growing through acquisition and growing from within," says Terry. Growing through acquisition involved buying synergistic contractors in other cities. Growing from within involved adding more people to handle more jobs, and training those people to move up in the organization and in their careers.

Gordon Lansford's rise through the ranks at J.E. Dunn provides a good example of the growth from within at the company. Gordon began working at J.E. Dunn in 1996 as an internal auditor but soon found his accounting skills put to use elsewhere. "I help Bob Long check the numbers on the companies

Dunn might buy. To estimate the value of a company, we have to look hard at its projected numbers to see how accurate they are. It's a time-consuming process, but it's also a lot of fun," Gordon says. He also works with Steve Dunn on insurance matters, bonding and prequalifying subcontractors. Now, his duties as senior vice president of finance for J.E. Dunn and vice president of finance for Dunn Industries include supervising a staff of 30 in the payroll, accounts payable, billings, and general accounting departments.

Gordon assisted Bob Long in the late 1990s when J.E. Dunn acquired C.E. Ward Constructors, Inc. of Houston (later renamed J.E. Dunn-Southwest). Later, J.E. Dunn ventured back into the

Colorado market, buying Hughes/ Smith, Inc., a Colorado Springs-based general contractor with about $40 million in annual revenues. Hughes/ Smith was renamed J.E. Dunn Rocky Mountain Region.

According to senior vice president Chuck Cianciaruso, acquiring existing companies follows the lessons learned about not getting "hometowned," and allows J.E. Dunn to compete on equal footing with local contractors. "Their ability to get work is a big factor because that determines their ability to be profitable and pay off the investment that Dunn Industries has made in them." He goes on to say that the companies' retention of their own flavor is a double-edged sword. "All of the marketing departments are different because they have been adapted to their market. Slowly, over a period of time, they get more and more like us, but they still have to adapt to their local area."

The expansions have led to a more national approach to marketing. "When you get outside of Kansas City," Cianciaruso continues, "it's a lot harder because we don't have those connections, so we send our marketing people to trade shows and other events where they develop contacts for markets such as hospitals, prisons, education, and high-tech."

In 2002, J.E. Dunn subsidiary R. J. Griffin completed the Metropolis, a 21-story, two-towered building in midtown Atlanta. It features 498 condominiums, six levels of parking, a health club for tenants, and leased retail space that fronts Peachtree Street.

Peter Doyle, president of J.E. Dunn-Southwest in Houston, notes that changes in marketing have been matched by changes in the field brought about by the opportunity of many skill sets and ways of doing business. "The company is spreading across the country because of the acquisitions. They are acquiring companies on the way up, not companies on the way down. Right now, we are doing two projects in Oklahoma City with Witcher Construction, one of our sister companies. I am making certain that we take advantage of our sister companies' strengths. Here in Houston, we want to piggyback on J.E. Dunn's health care expertise in Kansas City and Witcher's retail side."

Atlanta's R. J. Griffin & Company General Contractors, a firm which itself had expanded in recent years with offices in Nashville, Orlando, and Charlotte, N.C., represents Dunn Industries' most recent and largest acquisition. Announced in January of 2000, the R. J. Griffin & Company acquisition would significantly boost Dunn Industries revenues and create access to opportunities in the southeast. Jim Griffin founded R. J. Griffin & Company in 1985 after spending nearly 15 years working for one of Atlanta's largest contractors as a project manager and an executive. R. J. Griffin & Company's areas of operation in construction management, design/build, and preconstruction services dovetailed neatly with the other J.E. Dunn Group construction companies. The J.E. Dunn Group was able to extend its reach not only from coast to coast but from Canada to the Caribbean.

"Griffin has built their organization around customer satisfaction and strong relationships with their clients," says Terry. "One of the things that I've learned from Jim Griffin is that you have to decide who your preferred clients are and focus your efforts on getting and keeping their business."

Besides Jim Griffin, a few other standouts in Griffin's leadership are Steve Touchton, president; David Paris, executive

J.E. Dunn completed work on a five-level parking garage for the Double Eagle Hotel and Casino in Cripple Creek, Colo., in December 2003. Casino construction has provided steady work for J.E. Dunn in the last decade.

vice president who oversees its Atlanta, Nashville, and Florida operations; and Rick Sneed, executive vice president who is in charge of the Charlotte office.

"There is safety in geographical expansion," says Bob Long. "We can diversify geographically and we can still be in the construction business and somewhat tied to the construction cycle. At least when the activity in one area goes down, it's not necessarily the case that all areas will go down."

With a reference to earlier expansion efforts in other industries, he notes that, "Sticking with what we know is smart business and what we know is construction."

Training

*G*rowing from within, as Terry Dunn has indicated, is as critical as expansion, and such growth involves adding personnel and increasing skills.

Adding personnel began when Arnold Dreyer talked Ardyth Wendte into becoming the personnel director in the late 1970s, long before the term "human resources" was ever coined. The handful of people in the office and field personnel has grown steadily over the past 25 years, reaching 1,600 Kansas City employees by 2003. There are 350 people in the home

office and an average of 1,250 in the field. Overall, the J.E. Dunn Group, including its subsidiaries, averages 2,500 office and field employees.

Perhaps more important than numbers are skills. With all J.E. Dunn's specialties – high-tech, hospitals, prisons, renovation, schools, and offices – and new technologies every year, training has become an increasingly critical part of the enterprise. "Training is a way for J.E. Dunn to grow its own talent," says Steve Hamline.

The first serious training involving the superintendents began in the late 1970s with classes for Tom Turner, Jay Lucas, Kevin Shipley, Cliff Larson, Butch Bishop, Rusty Tuggle, and Vern Orpin. "Along with our training, we worked for the old school of general superintendents.

They trained us and in return we, as general superintendents, are training the next pool of general superintendents," says Vern Orpin.

Working under executive vice president Bernard Jacquinot, Cliff Larson, one of the early superintendent trainees and now a vice president, heads up J.E. Dunn's field operations. The summer intern program represents one of the primary entry points to J.E. Dunn. Cliff, who works with human resources

on the summer internship program, says the goal is to hire the best students and then get commitments from them during their senior year. "It's important for the summer interns to have a positive experience," he notes, "because they make

J.E. Dunn built new headquarters for the Heart of America United Way by renovating and connecting two old brick buildings in downtown Kansas City. J.E. Dunn continues to be one of the United Way's biggest supporters.

"We strive to be good corporate citizens," says Terry Dunn. "We believe in tithing and giving back both our money and our time to the community."

The Dunn Family Foundation is central to the Dunns' philanthropic activities. Bob Dunn is president and Bill Dunn Sr. is chairman. "It involves a lot of meetings and paperwork," says Bob. "It's allowed me to meet a lot of representatives from other foundations and learn what to look for in charitable requests. We get requests from more than 2,000 charities per year." J.E. Dunn philanthropic activities occasionally take another form – when jobs are undertaken at cost.

The Dunns also encourage employees to make their own personal commitments and be active volunteers. "One way we show our commitment to the community is in consistently being among the top corporate givers in the local United Way campaign," says Terry Dunn.

Phil Hanson, vice president for resource development of the Heart of America United Way, notes J.E. Dunn's high per capita employee involvement and hundreds of thousands raised for the United Way each year. "It is very unusual for a construction company to be so involved in the United Way." Individual J.E. Dunn employee gifts average as much as $655 per person.

And, finally, the Dunns and J.E. Dunn employees often serve on boards of charitable, civic and human service organizations. Randall O'Donnell, president and CEO of Children's Mercy Hospitals and Clinics, notes that "the Dunn family has a special involvement with the community. Bob Long is on the Board of Trustees for Children's Mercy Hospital and other J.E. Dunn employees are active in the Kansas City United Way program."

A central tenet of the J.E. Dunn organization is that 10 percent of pre-tax earnings is to be given to charities each year. When gifts-in-kind through reduced fees and services are counted, the figure is well in excess of 10 percent.

Before it constructed the Stowers Institute, J.E. Dunn first worked with Jim Stowers when it built twin towers for the company he founded, American Century Investments. The towers serve as nighttime beacons to the nearby Plaza shopping district in Kansas City.

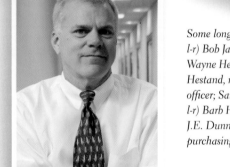

Some longtime employees of J.E. Dunn are: (top l-r) Bob Jacquinot, vice president-field operations; Wayne Heider, general superintendent; Billie Hestand, retired corporate secretary and J.E. Dunn officer; Sandy Comley, payroll manager; (bottom l-r) Barb Hachey, corporate secretary and officer of J.E. Dunn and Dunn Industries; and Ray Atkeisson, purchasing manager.

In 2001, the construction of a 30,000 square foot annex, known by its address, 901 Charlotte, across the street from Dunn's Holmes Street office, facilitated the task of fast-tracking employees into supervisory roles. The building contains classrooms and an audio-visual training center that allows employees and subcontractors to keep up on the newest means and methods of the construction business.

good entry level employees when they graduate from college."

"I recruit people who are committed to staying with us for 20 years," Cliff says. "Traditionally, it took seven to ten years to train someone for a supervisory position in the field." Cliff is trying to get that time reduced through an apprenticeship position that feeds right into a supervisory role.

New employees who want to be project managers also face years of training. Starting out as assistant project

managers, they pass through a variety of training levels over five years on their way to becoming senior project managers. Training begins with a summer "ambassador program," which introduces new hires to other employees, the company, and its culture. Their education continues over the next several years through a variety of multi-weekend programs that teach specific skills for project management such as dispute resolution, contract law, financial controls, and building fundamentals.

A Family Business

*T*he need for new employees, always critical in a growing company, has been mitigated to some extent over the years at J.E. Dunn by extraordinary loyalty. Not only have many employees remained with the company for ten, twenty, or thirty years, but some families have worked there for generations, just like the Dunns themselves.

For example, Bob Jacquinot, Bernard Jacquinot's son, has found his own important niche at J.E. Dunn. Bob worked as a project manager for a construction company in Houston before coming to J.E. Dunn where he started out in project management and helped develop some of the company's operational software. Like his father, Bob is involved in managing the field and warehouse operations. He also heads up J.E. Dunn's self-perform division, overseeing masonry, carpentry, and concrete work done by the construction company.

According to employees who have worked at J.E. Dunn the longest, the reason they stay has to do with the way they are treated. "I'll give 110 percent because they have taken care of me over the years," says superintendent Wayne Heider. "I think I owe them. They helped me when I had my back surgery and when my son had spinal meningitis. Mr. Dunn got the United Way to help for that."

Ray Malone, a longtime subcontractor, points out how J.E. Dunn's employee loyalty can benefit a client. "Their retention of employees brings a wealth of experience and knowledge to a project for their customers' benefit. Their work atmosphere allows them to retain employees. They have a 'Mom and Pop shop' attitude, instead of a big company attitude."

Part of treating employees right comes from sharing the wealth. Bill Sr. notes that the incentive bonus program he set up decades ago now distributes many millions of dollars per year to key employees. This sometimes averages out to two or three times an individual's salary. "It gives people all the benefits of being a stockholder without any of the liabilities," he says.

Of course, sometimes Bill Sr. has exceeded the recommendations of his staff in this regard. "Bill Dunn Sr. has a big heart for sure," says Dale Shikles. "He's good at intuitively making good decisions. During the bad years, he certainly paid bigger bonuses than I recommended he pay."

Steve Hamline sees the company's historic ability to retain quality employees as the key to J.E. Dunn's success over the years. "Our best assets are our people," he says.

Keeping Core Values Amid the Growth

*W*hether it was due to the people or the company's approach to business, J.E. Dunn grew by almost 400 percent in the 1990s. It reached revenues of $871 million by 1998, up from $686 million in 1997, and $220 million at the start of the decade. Five years later, with the acquisition of R. J. Griffin & Company, the revenues exceeded $1.6 billion, with over 2,500 employees working in 14 offices

nationwide and projects underway all over the country. Despite the economic slowdown that marked the first few years of the new millennium, the company continued to enjoy almost double-digit growth as a result of a substantial backlog of projects.

According to *Engineering News-Record* magazine, the J.E. Dunn Group ranked 25th out of the top 400 construction companies in terms of revenue in 2004. The J.E. Dunn Group also ranked among the top 25 in 14 specialty areas such as 6th in Construction

(top to bottom): Bill Jr., Terry, Steve, Kevin, and Bob Dunn continue the tradition of civic involvement begun by their grandfather, Ernie Dunn Sr.

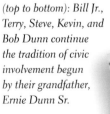
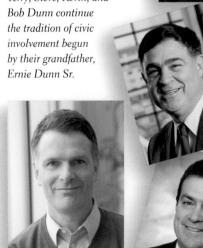

Management-at-Risk, 13th in commercial offices, 9th in education, 6th in health care, 6th in correctional facilities, and 3rd in religious and cultural.

Keeping with the core values of the company, the Dunn Family Foundation had donated millions of dollars over the same period to over 350 different organizations across a wide spectrum of churches, schools, hospitals, and civic programs. The Don Bosco Center, for example, which has been one of the largest recipients of the of the Dunn Family Foundation over the years, runs a counseling program, a charter school, a center for senior citizens, and many other programs. The organization, like so many others, has relied on funding from J.E. Dunn to meet the needs of the people it serves.

As with many local charities, the family's involvement with the Don Bosco Center began with Ernie Dunn Sr., who was on its board. After Ernie's death, Bill Sr. served on its board. Later both Bill Jr. and Bob served as chairmen.

Bill Sr. remains active in the community, serving on a variety of boards and commissions. Terry has assumed the most visible public roles, taking over in 1998 as vice chairman of the Federal Reserve Bank in Kansas City and in 2001 as chairman. He was also president of the Chamber of Commerce of Greater Kansas City, a position his father held almost a

quarter of a century before. "I hope to provide leadership as a facilitator, to help our community move ahead," he said upon accepting the position. "It takes a lot of time. It takes a lot of consensus-building."

In 2003, when Terry helped create the Superintendent's Roundtable, an organization that brings educators and business leaders together to encourage quality education in the Kansas City area, he had already shown his abilities in consensus-building, much as his father had done with the Labor Management Council.

In 1998, Steve Dunn was named chairman of the Downtown Council, a private nonprofit membership organization consisting of over 100 businesses, property owners, and organizations committed to the continued development of downtown Kansas City, Mo. Bill Jr. was chairman of the Kansas City, Kansas Chamber of Commerce and all five sons, including Kevin, have been active throughout the community helping hospitals, schools, and charities.

Remaining Private

*A*mong the most notable aspects of J.E. Dunn's 80-year history is the fact that it has remained a private, family-held company, when so many other similar firms in all industries

J.E. Dunn Construction general superintendent Rick Fortner.

allowed themselves to be acquired by larger public companies.

Larry Bingham, longtime general counsel, cites the importance of maintaining the values that built the company – taking care of the client, supporting the employees, serving the community – as central to the family's decision to retain control of the company. "Continued ownership is important. Once you sell it, you lose the cultural principles that Bill instilled in the company," said Larry.

Bill Sr. sees a philanthropic advantage to being family-owned. "I know that if we were a public corporation we would be having problems in giving away 10 percent of our pre-tax income each year to not-for-profit groups. If public corporations give away more than 1 percent, the shareholders object."

Steve Dunn, now chairman of J.E. Dunn Construction, also appreciates the latitude. "Unlike a publicly held company, we don't have to meet our profit projections every quarter to satisfy shareholders. We can reinvest more of our profit back into the business for future growth."

Employees, like safety director Jim D. Miller, are also glad to work for people they know and see all the time. "I have always liked the fact that I can tell somebody that I work for one of the largest companies in the United States, and it's family-owned," says Jim.

A Changing World

Chuck Cianciaruso points out one of the most fundamental changes for J.E. Dunn, one that reflects changes in society as a whole. "The jobs are more complicated and the clients are more complicated. That's what changed primarily about this business culturally."

The way J.E. Dunn markets itself has also changed dramatically, Cianciaruso adds. "We have evolved from Bill Sr. and Ardyth Wendte doing the marketing part-time to 18 people working solely on marketing, public relations, graphics, and business development."

Reliance on computers was a change noticed by Rick Fortner, who appreciates computers from the superintendent's perspective: "With the old method, you'd physically tape off the site when you laid out a building. Now we use programs

Projects like the Nelson-Atkins Museum expansion challenge J.E. Dunn to turn architects' dreams into reality.

in the computer to lay out the jobs. Computers also help with scheduling and with a daily diary. They're great for keeping track of the subcontractor list."

Bill Dunn Jr., the company's equipment guru, uses tower cranes as an example of changes in technology. "The computer age and software packages have made the equipment more sophisticated. The tower cranes now have computers aboard them that monitor all the systems. The equipment now is more operator-friendly; however,

it requires a more highly-trained mechanic because of the computerized controls and software."

The sophistication of the equipment and the gains the labor unions won in the 1970s and 1980s have turned some standard equations upside-down in the construction industry. "The rising cost of labor versus what it used to be is the biggest change," says Hamline. "[It used to be] cheap labor and expensive material. It's different now. The roles have been reversed."

Senior Vice President Casey Halsey and Sabra Sandy, assistant secretary and officer of J.E. Dunn and Dunn Industries.

Dan West, vice president notes that new materials, particularly concrete materials, spur architects' imaginations. "Because of new materials, architectural firms are creating things that have never been created. We are working with Steven Holl Architects on the Nelson-Atkins Museum and they have people there who are dreaming the next dream. This creates new challenges for us. There are always going to be new challenges as we go, but that keeps work interesting."

Over time, new priorities bring a change in procedures. Retired general superintendent Dick Neumann recognizes J.E. Dunn's safety standards as "one of the most significant changes that has happened to J.E. Dunn. When I started in 1945, we took lots of chances and did lots of things wrong. We used wood scaffolding

that had knots in it and would break. Now there are laminated planks; they are much stronger, much better. Now there are guardrails. In the past, you could walk anywhere on a two by four and no one would say anything. You could ride on the top of a crane and you can't do that today. You can't do this and you can't do that. Safety is the biggest change at J.E. Dunn Construction and I think it's good."

Longtime safety director Jim D. Miller has been the architect of many of the safety initiatives. "I'm proud of the way our program has evolved. It is now basically above and beyond OSHA's requirements. I'm proud of the fact that all of our foremen and superintendents hold 10-hour OSHA certificates. All are trained in first aid and CPR."

Insurance in the construction industry has grown more complex over the years. "When I was handling safety issues, I learned about the insurance part of the job," says Steve Dunn. "I dealt with worker's comp, general liability, and property insurance. At one time I handled all the employee

benefits such as health insurance, life insurance, and really the whole gamut of insurance coverage in the workplace."

"I still oversee much of this, such as insurance for bonding," continues Steve, "but today there are more people who are really hands-on with it. In the employee benefits area, Rick Beyer handles that and he works with the different insurance agents whether it's health care, disability, or life insurance. As far as the claims handling, which I used to do by myself, Sabra Sandy now handles a lot of that, e.g., automobile claims, builders' risk claims. Sabra has done a great job with that and she can handle about any claim that comes around. Some of the claims can get pretty difficult. Then attorneys Tom Whittaker, Casey Halsey, Phil Donnellan or I will assist her." The three in-house attorneys work primarily on contracts, subcontractors' claims, and licenses.

Lawsuits have been rare at J.E. Dunn. Casey Halsey explains how J.E. Dunn has kept its court appearances to a minimum. "We're fortunate in Kansas City that we have good subcontractors that know us well and who feel like we've treated them fairly enough that litigation isn't usually an issue. For the construction companies that J.E. Dunn has acquired, we've worked hard to make them subcontractor-friendly on the premise that we rely on subcontractors to have a successful job." Casey gives a lot of credit to Bill Dunn Sr. "I learned early on from him that it's more important to resolve the issue and live to build another day than it is to be right and collect every last penny of what you're owed. Bill's approach has been to find a reasonable middle ground, get the matter resolved, and go on."

New Leadership and a New Look

*T*he beginning of a new century has brought additional administrative changes. In January 1999, Bill Dunn Sr. retired as chairman of Dunn Industries, Inc. in favor of Bob Long. Steve Dunn was named vice chairman, and Bill Jr. became executive vice president. Terry remained president and CEO of Dunn Industries and J.E. Dunn Construction, and Bob Dunn stayed on as vice president of both Dunn Industries and J.E. Dunn Construction. A little more than a year later, in March of 2000, Bill Dunn Sr. stepped down from his chairman post at J.E. Dunn Construction and turned over the reins to Steve.

Making up for the leadership gap at the top resulting from Bill Dunn's final departure from day-to-day activities, retired Army Lt. General Jack Nix Jr. was brought in as chief operating officer and executive vice president of J.E. Dunn Contruction. His responsibilities as COO, a newly created position, include oversight for project management, field operations, warehouse operations, construction planning and quality assurance for five J.E. Dunn offices, including the one in Kansas City. Jack sees many similarities between his experience in the Army and his position at J.E. Dunn. "Much of my work at J.E. Dunn involves training people and moving people and material from one assignment to the next, much like a

(above) Jack Nix, chief operating officer and executive vice president.

(left) High-tech meets historic preservation when J.E. Dunn converted the First National Bank into the Kansas City Library.

logistics system in the military. In both the U.S. Army and at J.E. Dunn, there's a lot of value placed on trust and integrity."

Building into the Future

*A*s the middle part of a new decade approaches, J.E. Dunn remains extremely busy with the usual school, hospital, and commercial projects. Across the country it is at work in 44 states, and in Kansas City it retains a high profile with work such as the renovation of the Commerce Trust Building, the transformation of the historic First National Bank Building into the Kansas City Library, and the addition to the Nelson-Atkins Museum of Art.

The historic preservation of the stately First National Bank building represents the centerpiece of an effort to revitalize the neighborhood surrounding 10th and Baltimore. High-tech and restoration come together in the old bank building – where tellers once manually counted money – with the installation of public access computers, an adaptive technology center for customers with special needs and a learning center for continuing education.

The Nelson-Atkins is perhaps the signature building of the new decade in

A drawing shows the five irregular structures, sometimes called "lenses," that will glow above 140,000 square feet of new exhibition space at the Nelson-Atkins Museum.

its audacity and extraordinary architecture. It features five irregular structures, sometimes called "lenses," designed to glow above 140,000 square feet of new underground exhibition space. The lenses will be constructed of special glass run in production only once a year in Germany and tested at special facilities in Florida. The design includes a garage with an undulating concrete ceiling and a reflecting pool. The $130 million-plus project will not be completed until 2005. General superintendent Steve Hoye has

several assistant superintendents working on the project that nearly encircles the existing museum.

The Nelson-Atkins addition is the current version of, as Dan West puts it, "someone dreaming the next dream." And J.E. Dunn is, once again, the dream weaver.

J.E. Dunn recently renovated the historic 1907 Commerce Trust Building in downtown Kansas City. The fully refurbished lobby is pictured.

Epilogue

A LEGACY FOR TOMORROW

*The Deramus Education Pavilion, part of J.E. Dunn's
construction project at the Kansas City Zoo in the 1990s.*

THE FUTURE

The Challenges and Opportunities of Expansion

BETWEEN SIXTY AND SEVENTY YEARS AGO J.E. DUNN CON-STRUCTION WAS STRUGGLING TO ESTABLISH ITSELF AND FIND ITS NICHE. THIRTY YEARS AGO, SURVIVAL WAS THE ISSUE. BY THE EARLY 1980S, GROWTH HAD SUPERCEDED SURVIVAL AS A PRIORITY, BUT, LIKE ALL CHANGE, GROWTH NOW REPRESENTS A CHALLENGE TO THE EXISTING CULTURE.

*A*s the company grows, the office people don't have as much time to see their projects going on in the field," reflects Bob Long. "It takes a lot of the fun away; you are farther away from seeing the creation of your efforts. It removes some of the feel of it. Other than that, you don't

J.E. Dunn Northwest established a foothold in the far north, completing the Valdez Hospital in Alaska during the summer of 2004.

know as many people. It isn't the same kind of environment as when you could sit everyone around a table and discuss things. Problems with communication are greater and probably even more important, and you have to learn to manage people rather than things. There's a lot of change that size brings."

Terry Dunn is extremely mindful of the consequences of change and growth. "When I worked for the company in the 1980s," he says, "I knew the names and backgrounds of all the foremen and the

superintendents. Today, in just Kansas City, we have close to 70 superintendents and a couple hundred foremen, and I don't know them all by their first names. When you add the subsidiaries, we literally have 200 to 250 superintendents working for our company and 300 to 400 foremen. Today we have close to 2,700 employees."

How does he manage a situation so drastically different than the one his father faced? "I don't try to know every individual. What I try to do is know and understand the leadership that is providing

R. J. Griffin & Company built the Cleveland Regional Medical Center in Shelby, N.C.

direction among the employees. You have to empower others to provide leadership."

Like any good field marshal, new COO Jack Nix recognizes that victory depends on those troops who are now too numerous to name, but on whose skill the future of the company depends. "We use any current market downtime," he says, "to consolidate our gains by refining training programs, developing better processes and providing our great people with opportunities in other markets. The key to our future, as in the past, will be our ability to recruit and train quality people who embody the values the Dunn family established. Done well, this will make J. E. Dunn the national, preferred contractor."

Despite the dangers of impersonalization, expansion remains a priority for the future. "In order for this company to grow," says Steve Dunn, "we will need to go out of town. We have to be willing to travel to meet the needs of the big clients. I think the synergies that develop among us and our acquired companies are going to help our national growth."

(left) The Minneapolis Institute of Arts, a project built by J.E. Dunn Group company, Witcher Construction Co.

(opposite) J.E. Dunn boosted Kansas City's claim as "The City of Fountains" when it built the Ewing and Muriel Kauffman Memorial Garden, one of several fountain sights the construction company has added to the cityscape in recent years.

Now that J.E. Dunn is savvy about how to expand, synergy is an important word. Not only does the market have to be ripe and the potential subsidiary's local reputation solid, but the corporate culture has to be one that J.E. Dunn can assimilate. "The first thing we look at is reputation," says Terry. "We also look at the financial performance, the people, and how that company relates to its clients to see if it's compatible with J.E. Dunn. The work I do now is very people-intensive in trying to recruit, train, and develop people and help them to grow. When I look at a subsidiary, I'm really looking at the people component and the chemistry within that entity to grow and allow its people to reach their fullest potential."

The Kansas City office has learned, however, that it cannot impose the J.E. Dunn culture wholesale. "We've empowered CEOs at the J.E. Dunn Group companies in hopes that they will lead with an entrepreneurial spirit, grow their operations, and be accountable for their results," said Terry. "We learned quickly that we can provide direction and support, but we have to allow the heads of the subsidiaries to provide the leadership."

For Bob Long, whose Dunn Industries oversees all the Group companies, the list of additional concerns with expansion is long. "I worry about the quality of our work. I worry about whether or not we are still putting owners first. I worry that we don't ever move away from that principle of fairness. Treating people fairly doesn't mean that we're easy. Not at all. But we're fair and if we screw something up, we'll fix it and we're not going to charge the client for it."

The hope is that subsidiaries bring more benefits than worries, not just in revenues but in referrals and expanded capabilities.

"We're spreading our market, offering opportunities for people to grow in the business, and we're also cross marketing," says Terry. "In 2002 we recognized probably $100 million worth of work that was referred by one subsidiary to another. That number from cross marketing will probably grow to 20 percent to 25 percent of our work. Each of the subsidiaries can learn and grow by drawing on the history and experiences of the other subsidiaries, particularly where we have senior leadership in specific areas."

One of the plans, says Steve Dunn, is to focus on each company's strength. "We might take the lead in hospitals in Kansas City, Witcher in Minneapolis might handle a retail project, and we'd look to J.E. Dunn-Northwest, in Portland for an entertainment facility."

Like his brothers, Steve feels "the sky's the limit, but we must continue to attract the very best people and instill in them the J.E. Dunn culture: ethics, commitment, a focus on satisfied customers."

If maintaining the corporate culture is one challenge, keeping the company private and under family control could be an even bigger one. According to Bill Jr., "family members who've paid the price by getting the required skills, training, and education, and [who have] shown an ability to get along with employees and lead aggressively, will have the opportunity to lead."

Bob, who runs the Dunn Family Foundation, thinks about maintaining traditional J.E. Dunn values. "We would like to be recognized in every community where we have an office as one of the top local corporate philanthropists. We feel it's important to give back to the community. The challenge will be building up our philanthropic image in new cities that we've entered."

The plan, he says, is to simply keep on giving. "We will always stick to our giving philosophy, considering requests that focus on education, economic development, health and human services, youth, senior programs, and religious and minority programs."

Niches

J.E. Dunn has established itself in a variety of areas, from hospitals to prisons to high-tech to church work, but other niches remain in such areas as environmental or heavy industrial work. Ever wary of venturing too far from core competencies, Terry is currently focused on improving the communication and synergies between the subsidiaries. "We've done a good job of projecting business, keeping ahead of the wave. We're seeing opportunities in high-tech, biotech, research, churches, housing, retirement housing – things of that nature. Ten years ago, some of these areas weren't even on our radar screen. New niche markets could allow us to double or triple our size within the next seven to eight years," he says.

Terry is also looking at the future with a wider vision. "The construction industry is actually made up of many areas that have their own cycles. In many circumstances, the cycles sometimes run against each other. What J.E. Dunn needs to be doing is looking ahead to see what way the stronger cycles are going, what the emerging demographic issues are, and what technology changes will impact our business for many, many years."

Prognostication is a challenge, but the tools for it are improving. "I don't know if the construction industry will ever be able to look more than two to three years ahead, but that's still an improvement on how it once was when six to nine months was about as far out as we could project. Information technology and a very active marketing department have allowed us to broaden that horizon."

A Legacy to Take Into the Future

*I*t is difficult, if not impossible, to encapsulate a legacy of over 80 years. Perhaps it rests in the skyline of Kansas City, or now other communities across the country, where J.E. Dunn cranes and skyscrapers have scratched the heavens.

Snowcapped mountains provide the backdrop for Pine Creek High School in Colorado Springs. J.E. Dunn built the technology magnet school in 1998 and is currently adding an academic wing.

Maybe it is in the ability to survive and grow as a family-owned corporation in an era of conglomerates, or in the way J.E. Dunn has fostered loyalty among generations of employees. Perhaps the legacy is in the projects J.E. Dunn has undertaken without profit, from the Quartermaster Depot to the Hyatt restoration or the countless civic contributions it has made.

Given Bill Sr.'s service in the military and all the Dunns' affinity for football and coaching, it makes sense to look to an old football coach from West Point to best define the achievement, and legacy, of J.E. Dunn. "Leadership," said legendary Army Coach Paul Dietzel, "is the ability to lift and inspire."

Dave Lockton, president of the Lockton companies, notes how J.E. Dunn has led and inspired others in Kansas City. "I got to know the Dunns through industry and civic endeavors, especially the United Way. Dunn changed the commitment of the whole construction industry to worthy causes, especially the subcontractor industry. They made general contractors compete with them for civic recognition and they have made subcontractors better citizens within our community."

Of course, leadership is not possible without the success that three generations of Dunns have fostered since the early 1920s. And it is incumbent on the current generation to carry forward the legacy of success that made J.E. Dunn the most respected general contractor in Kansas City and one of the fastest growing such firms in the nation.

Jim Griffin, a general superintendent, sums up the J.E. Dunn legacy. "I know that the Dunn family's goal is to be the best," he says. "The best I like."

J.E. Dunn built a new corporate headquarters for Kansas City Southern in downtown Kansas City in 2002.

ENDNOTES

[1] Kansas City Star, About Town column August 16, 1966.
[2] Kansas City Star, May 24, 1943.
[3] Kansas City Star, January 3, 1943.
[4] Kansas City Star, February 20, 1949 "It Happened in Kansas City."
[5] Kansas City Times, Ocotber 4, 1948.
[6] Kansas City Star, May 28, 1950.
[7] Kansas City Star, January 29, 1954.
[8] Kansas City Star, August 26, 1962.
[9] Kansas City Star, September 14, 1969.
[10] Kansas City Star, July 25, 1969.
[11] Kansas City Times, April 2, 1969.
[12] Kansas City Star, July 14, 1969.
[13] Kansas City Times, July 29, 1969.
[14] Kansas City Times, August 2, 1969.
[15] Kansas City Times, March 24, 1970.
[16] Kansas City Times, February 24 1970.
[17] Kansas City Star, August 20, 1970.
[18] Kansas City Times, July 6, 1973.
[19] Kansas City Star, June 17, 1974.
[20] Kansas City Times, January 24, 1976.
[21] Kansas City Star, April 11, 1976.
[22] The Kansas City Star, May 19, 1972.
[23] Kansas City Star, May 13, 1984.

PHOTO CREDITS

At the Kansas City Library Garage, the classics loom large.

PHOTO CREDITS CONTINUED

KEVIN DUNN

THE J.E. DUNN STORY: BUILDING FROM THE HEART IS PART BUSINESS BIOGRAPHY, PART FAMILY HISTORY FOR CO-AUTHOR KEVIN DUNN, GRANDSON OF THE CONSTRUCTION COMPANY'S FOUNDER, JOHN ERNEST DUNN. KEVIN RECEIVED A LAW DEGREE FROM THE UNIVERSITY OF KANSAS AND LATER EARNED A MASTER'S DEGREE IN PROFESSIONAL WRITING FROM THE UNIVERSITY OF MISSOURI-KANSAS CITY. *THE J.E. DUNN STORY* IS HIS FIRST PUBLISHED BOOK.

TROUPE NOONAN

TROUPE NOONAN IS A JOURNALIST AND HISTORIAN. HE HAS WRITTEN FOR MAJOR MAGAZINES SUCH AS *LIFE*, *FORBES FYI*, AND IN-FLIGHT MAGAZINES FOR 25 YEARS. THE AUTHOR OR GHOSTWRITER OF A NUMBER OF CUSTOM BOOKS FOR FAMILIES, INDIVIDUALS AND BUSINESSES, HE IS PRESIDENT OF HERITAGE HISTORIES, PUBLISHERS OF CUSTOM BOOKS.

The Cerner Corporation, a leader in health care software, has hired J.E. Dunn for several building projects at its headquarters campus in North Kansas City.

INDEX

References to illustrations and photographs
    are in boldface.